ARMAMENT AND TECHNOLOGY

HELICOPTERS

Ilustrations: Octavio Díez Cámara, Northrop Grumman Corporation, Agusta, McDonnell Douglas Corp., AATD, F. Nebinger-CEV/Matra, Eurocopter, GIAT Industries, Matra BaE Dynamics, FN Herstal, Rostvertol Company, Litton, Kongsberg, MAPO, ITT Defense and Electronics, NHI Industries, British Aerospace y Antonio Ros Pau.

Production: Ediciones Lema, S.L.
Editor: Josep M. Parramón Homs
Text: Octavio Díez
Coordination: Victoria Sánchez and Eduardo Hernández
Translation: Brian Menzies

© Ediciones Lema, S.L. 1998

I.S.B.N. 84-95323-16-8

Photocomposition and photomechanics: Novasis, S.A.L.
Barcelona (Spain)
Printed in Spain

ARMAMENT AND TECHNOLOGY

HELICOPTERS

LEMA
Publications

Designed as a helicopter with the ability to neutralize multiple surface targets, the "Apache" had its baptism of fire in the Gulf War where its features were demonstrated in the destruction of a good part of the Iraqi mechanized columns and armor, as it also did with the neutralization of other targets such as command posts, anti-aircraft systems, communication systems and a long list of others which gave us proof of its capability as a combat vehicle.

Facing the threat

The importance of the large and growing concentration of armored vehicles in the now extinct Warsaw Pact, was the reason for the United States developing an airfleet to break its hypothetical advance.

The Conception

After Lockheed´s "Cheyenne" AH56A program was cancelled and the attack missions during the Vietnam conflict were left to the Bell AH-1 "Cobra", which demons-

---

THE LONGBOW APACHE

Chosen by the armies of the United States, United Kingdom and the Netherlands, the AH-64D is the most modern version of the "Apache" multi-mission helicopter and incorporates various improvements in a number of its sensors, its weapon capacity and cockpit design, increasing its ability to act when facing all kinds of targets.

THE CAVALRY

Various squadrons of United States cavalry use "Apache" attack helicopters for operations from carrying out reconnaissance missions to others of mass destruction.

---

trated weaknesses when carrying out some missions, the requirements for the AAH (Army Advanced Attack Helicopter) program were formulated. After investigating various proposals a contract was signed on the 22nd of June 1973 with Hughes Helicopters and Bell Helicopter Textron, which respectively proposed their YAH-64 and YAH-63 models, of which the first would be chosen, going into flight on the 30th of September 1975. Following a long period of development time, and after modifications to constituent parts, the first model of the series left the factory in September 1983 and was delivered to the United States Army the next year; on the 26th of January 1984.

Production

Contracted in the 1982 budget, the first 11 operational models were added to the 6 prototypes (one for ground trials, and five flight-worthy models), the deliveries allowing the needs to be met of the crew training center in Fort Rucker (Alabama) and also those of specific training centers in areas such as maintenance, logistics, avionics etc. The third squadron of the 6th cavalry regiment became the first unit to reach operational readiness in July 1986.

After orders for a total of 827 "Apaches" and a production rate that has allowed the manufacture of more than a hundred machines a year, the last (the 'A' model) was delivered on the 30th of April 1996 to one of the 35 air cavalry squadrons equipped with this model. Others also with this model include the National Guard, with seven, and the Reserve with two. The decision to increase the

number of helicopters in each battalion from 18 to 24 has meant that from 1997 there are 26 units operating with the AH-64A.

The Improvements

Despite the improvements made to the original design, such as the ability to employ the M230 cannon ("Chain Gun") in air to air combat. The possibility of employing "Stinger" or "Mistral" infra-red missiles for self defence against other armed equipment or to shoot down slow flying planes and helicopters; the introduction of a global positioning system (GPS); anti-interference radios ("Singars") or the adoption of an integrated electronic warfare system, it was decided in August 1990 to begin updating the helicopter, resulting in the AH-64D Longbow Apache.

The features of the new version have been validated by evaluating the working of various prototypes, of which the first flew on the 15th of April 1992. An agreement was made in 1996 to make 232 machines up to the year 2000 and in March 1997 the delivery began of the first AH-64Ds manufactured by McDonnell Douglas, the company which now manages production. A period of ten years is forecast to transform the 758 machines that make up the existing fleet.

Capacity

After requests for more than two hundred new or army surplus models from Israel, Saudi Arabia, Egypt, Greece, The United Arab Emirates, The Netherlands or The United Kingdom, which manufactures them under licence, the forecasted number to be built is 1,040 which can be added to requests from a variety of other countries showing an interest in the United States attack machine. These countries include Kuwait, Malaysia, Singapore, Sweden, South Korea or Spain, which were hoping to acquire thirty attack helicopters for its Helicopter Attack Battalion (BHELA).

An advanced design

With a robust configuration that improves its performance and capacity the "Apache" has been designed on advanced lines that increase the likelihood of the survival of the pilot and co-pilot/weapon operator. The range of possible weapons has increased, it has a high resistance to impacts from light weapons and anti-aircraft fire and it acquits itself well in accidents or ground crashes at speeds up to 12.8 metres per second. This is thanks to its landing carriage or undercarriage which has a high capacity for absorbing impacts.

Both crew members travel in a heavily armored double cockpit, which resists armor piercing missiles of dimensions up to 12.7x99mm and they have at their disposition a variety of systems to carry out their activities, such as flight helmets with integrated data displays and guidance systems, multi-functional cockpit display screens and a wide range of equipment that includes the

Doppler Plessey AN/ASN - 157 navigator, a digital auto-stabilizer, and a navigation system that combines a radar altimeter, laser, aerial data, INS, Doppler, and GPS.

The 1,890 horsepower of each of the two GET700-GE701C jet engines, mounted on each side of the fuselage give it great agility and the ability for the helicopter to acquit itself well in multiple operations. The jet engines are covered with armored plating ,which act as maintenance platforms. The radius of operation is limited by the fuel, a total of 1,421 litres that can be carried in four additional external tanks, from the Brunswick Corporation, with a capacity of 871 litres each. With a high level of protection a helicopter can fly for 30 minutes after being hit by 12.7mm projectiles in any part of the fuselage, although in some zones it can resist 23mm. Its transmission can continue working for an hour even though there is no lubricating oil.

Combat

The most modern version of this Uni-

SPECIALIZATION

Its power, capability, and possibilities of attack have made the AH-64 the reference by which later attack helicopter designs are measured.

CANON

Installed below the fuselage, guided automatically towards its objective by sensors and fed by a considerable ammunition supply, the 30mm M230 canon, the "Chain Gun", can fire at a rate of 625 rounds a minute and its effectiveness is striking against all types of armored vehicles and targets.

---

ted States helicopter is capable of working equally well at night as it is during the day, or in adverse weather conditions, for which it is equipped with laser, infra-red and other high technology systems that allow it to detect, classify and prioritize targets. It then tracks and attacks them. The first activities involve the use of the Westinghouse Radar which is capable of presenting up to 256 targets on the tactical positioning screen. This is mounted on the mast above the main rotor. This is an acquisition system from Lockheed Martin Orlando Aerospace with the joint TADS/PNVS which has an infra-red sensor

presenting a thermal image of the point being observed and an integrated counter-measure system- SN/ALQ-211SIRFC (Suite of Integrated RF Countermeasures) which complements the warning alarm sys-

tem for the detection of radar and laser emissions, the infra-red interference system AN/ALQ-144 and rocket launchers M-130 acting as decoy flares. British helicopters substituted the SIRFC for a GEC-Marconi HIDAS system (Integrated Defence Aids System).

Attack missions are entrusted to the McDonnel Douglas automatic canon, the machine gun, which is capable of firing 30mm bullets at a rate of 625 rounds per minute, fed by a magazine of 1,200 rounds. There are two stub wings with four attachments which can hold 16 Hellfire anti-tank RF missiles, 2.75 inch flare rockets, air to air missiles with infra-red guidance systems, Sidearm anti-radar missiles etc. All of these allow it to act as an armed escort, hunter or attack helicopter.

ROTOR

The asymmetric four-bladed tail rotor is located on the left side of the machine in a way which optimizes and stabilizes the agile movements of this attack helicopter.

PROPULSION

Installed on the sides of the fuselage and with quick release panels to facilitate maintenance work, the two GE T700- GE-701C jet engines together deliver 3,780 horsepower and incorporated in the outlet there is a nozzle which reduces its own infra-red signature making it difficult to locate.

SHOCK ABSORPTION

A small wheel is incorporated below the tail with a shock absorption system which prevents the back section of the fuselage from touching the ground during hard landings when being employed in combat duties.

WINGS

On the side of the fuselage there are two stub wings with two attachments for the location of weapons like Hellfire anti-tank missiles, rocket launchers or auxiliary fuel tanks.

RADAR

The Longbow variant incorporates a Westinghouse radar in a semi-spherical housing located above the main rotor, with the function of locating targets and optimizing the guidance of weapons in the attack.

COCKPIT

The AH-64D has improved the work possibilities of the pilot and co-pilot with the implementation of cockpit control systems which now give multi-function display screens and have increased the time available for doing other activities.

SENSORS

A stabilized gyro is located in the front nose which guides the thermal sensors and laser during flight, including in adverse conditions, enabling the use of the onboard weapons.

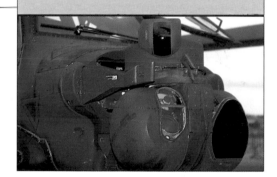

AH-64D TECHNICAL CHARACTERISTICS

COST:	18 million dollars	Fuel, external	3,484 l
DIMENSIONS:		**PROPULSION:**	
Length	15.47 m	Two GE T700-GE-701C jet engines with a total	
Height	4.95 m	of 3,780 horsepower	
Width	5.227 m	**PERFORMANCE:**	
Main rotor turning area	168.11 m²	Service ceiling height	6,400 m
Tail rotor turning area	6.13 m²	Stationary ceiling height	4,115 m
WEIGHT:		Maximum speed	261 km/h
Empty	5,352 kg	Range	407 km
Maximum	10,107 kg	Extended range	1,899 km
Maximum external load	2,712 kg	Design factor loading	+3.5/-0.5 g's
Fuel, internal	1,421 l		

The BO-105 has been used for surveillance tasks by the police in the cities of New York and Barcelona; and carrying out anti-tank missions in the German and Swedish armies. Patroling the straits of Gibraltar with the Spanish Coastguard and on patrolin the coastal waters of Mexico and Chile. The small BO-105 has shown its flexibility to adapt itself to varied assignments and realize a variety of missions in a civil, police or military capacity.

Evolution

Set up after the Second World War as a multi-national company, the firm Messerschmidt-Bölkow-Blohm (MBB) began the design of helicopters with the training model BO-102 which they followed by developing the BO-103 and BO-104.

Development

Despite the failure of some of the earlier models, such as an the observation two-seater that did not go into production, it was decided to go ahead with the construction of the multi-purpose twin-engine civil BO-105, with the second prototype flying on the 16th of February 1967. It was

provided with the four-blade rotor of the Westland Scout British helicopter, after the first prototype was destroyed during land-based trials.

The good prospects for the C civil version encouraged the German army to test its features out against other similar models, and it was chosen in 1974, in its repowered CB form, to carry out reconnaissance tasks, and in 1975, as the tank hunter PAH-1. At the same time as the two

hundred German models were received, a process that lasted until 1984, orders began to arrive from other nations that saw their requirements satisfied by this machine.

Exports

The Spanish army received some models transferred by the German army and decided to incorporate about eighty machines in their different versions of: observation, direct support, and anti-tank. These were produced under licence by Construcciones Aeronáuticas SA (CASA) in their factory in Getafe. In this plant a good proportion of the fifty plus models constructed were exported to Iraq. These were actively employed in the years of its war with Iran. They were used as weapon carrier platforms for HOT missiles attacking Iranian Chieftain and M-60 tanks.

As such, at the end of 1984 Sweden chose it as the platform for the Saab-Emerson

SMALL
Its small size and flight possibilities allow it to take advantage the of ruggedness of terrain and woodland formations to elude enemy vigilance and strike its targets without danger of being shot down.

POLICE USE
The forces of the Spanish Civil Guard employ the BO-105 helicopters in police surveillance tasks, the transport of special groups like the Special Intervention Unit (UEI) and the Rural Action Group (GAR), and in the patrol of sensitive areas.

/TOW system, and was established with orders arriving from, amongst others, Colombia, Brunei, Indonesia, The Netherlands, Canada, Mexico, The Philippines, Peru, Nigeria, Chile and South Korea. Some of the 1,300 models that serve in some forty countries were assembled or manufactured under licence in the Chilean plant of Enaer, the Indonesian IPTN, the Canadian company Eurocopter Canada and the Korean Daewoo Heavy Industries.

Excellent Possibilities

The features of this model and its agility make it suitable for carrying out certain special missions that do not need a high cargo capacity. For police use, its low noise level is very useful for patrolling in cities. It can drop in special group personnel who travel hung from its skids, in pairs on each side, until they reach their mission zones. Meanwhile, for military type tasks it can carry out VIP transport missions and link between different positions for the transport of small loads or groups of up to three people. Also exploration of land and sea areas, armed reconnaissance to act against hostile elements or tank-hunting to stop the advance of armoured formations and mechanised enemy forces among many other possibilities of tactical employment.

From the special versions, the Navy

models stand out which, like the Mexican version, incorporate a search radar in the nose and a winch for hoisting small loads, which are very useful features for air-sea rescue of fishing vessel crews, recreational sailing crews or military units. On this type of mission the helicopter increases its operational range with an optional fuel tank which is located in the passenger transport area, as used by the Colombian Navy.

Design

Conceived as a compact unit and easily maintained, the BO-105 continues to offer its services to a wide range of locations and in the hands of many users its ease of

NAVAL

The Chilean, Colombian and Mexican navies employ the BO-105 navy model, which like this Chilean example, includes a detector radar, skids with emergency floats, a small cargo winch and other modifications for its sea missions.

ARMED

The armed model is specified by the Spanish Army. It has a 20mm Rheinmetall RH-202 cannon underneath the fuselage, fed by a magazine located in the transport area, all of which has necessitated higher skids.

piloting stands out, although its power is limited for some operations.

Configuration

The fuselage is one element, with the cockpit occupying the front part, the engines the back, and the tail beam carrying the tail-rotor. The two pilots are housed in the front part of the cockpit and work with a central console in the form of a "T". This contains the instruments showing engine and flight equipment data, and offers very good visibility with a large window up front which includes two wipers.

Behind this is a three seater bench which can be removed to transport small cargo,

LAUNCHER
The anti-tank model has triple launchers on the side which can house up to three guided HOT missiles which can strike all types of targets within a 2.5 mile radius.

Propulsion

The engine in the CB model consists of two Allison 250-C20B jet engines which have a maximum power of 800HP, although if necessary performance of up to 850HP can be obtained. Each engine weighs 70.3 kilograms, has a rotation speed of 6,016 rpm and is designed to use different types of aviation fuel. The Allisons are isolated by a titanium fire-proof bulkhead and they incorporate automatic freon gas extinguishing equipment.

Connected to these, there is a rotor with special characteristics, designed with a titanium head and four reinforced plas-

with a hold in the rear part, which can be reached through two rear doors, where complementary equipment, spares, or the crew's own equipment is normally carried. The elongated tail is a semi-monohull cons-

truction, manufactured in light alloy; its rear part has two tailplanes and a tail which includes the rotor with the job of providing maximum lateral stability.

Located in the lower part of the fuselage are the two skids that form the landing gear, constructed out of metal tubes with plastic parts that can deform on contact with the ground, while the anti-tank models incorporate a side mounting fixed to the fuselage so missiles can be carried.

ANTI-TANK
Almost fifty machines make up the anti-tank group assigned to the 1st Battalion Attack Helicopters (BHELA) of the Spanish Army; its main armament consists of the long-range guided HOT missile, with armor piercing capacity.

tic blades. Each has a working life of 10,000 hours, or 200 after being pierced by light arms projectiles. They are joined to the head without any type of damping. This very rigid structure has the advantage of being made from far fewer pieces than other more sophisticated units, which greatly facilitates maintenance tasks, eases the execution of negative-G manoeuvres, and offers an immediate response to the controls.

The fuel tanks are incorporated below the floor of the main cockpit and they are filled through a fixed intake located in the rear part of the left-hand side. They have a total capacity of 570 litres. This can be increased by 200 litre auxiliary tanks that can be situated in the rear cargo hold.

Tank-hunting

Acting as the main aerial anti-tank element of the German and Spanish armies, this helicopter has been adapted to complete this kind of mission with the highest guarantees of success. Therefore, an SFIM APX M397 girostabilised viewfinder has been incorporated. This has been fixed to the upper part of the cockpit in a way that, from his seat, the system operator can capture the targets, be they static or mobile, and guide the missile automatically, only needing to keep the object in the cross of the visor.

Choosing the target, he can fire one of the six second-generation long-range HOT heavy anti-tank missiles, located on the triple side mountings, that have a range of up to four thousand metres and can pierce heavily armored NATO targets. The launcher functions as long as maneuvres do not exceed a turning radius of six degrees per second and a vertical movement of 45°. The Swedish models can carry out the same mission. These are armed with guided TOW anti-tank missiles from the United States.

Equipment

On specific models, like those of the

> **EXPLORATION**
> Through its small size and low noise level, the BO-105 can successfully perform reconnaissance and exploration missions before land forces go into action.

Spanish Military, a Rheimetall RH-202 20mm automatic cannon has been sited on the underside of the fuselage.

This is fed by a magazine located in the fuselage transport area. It can fire controlled bursts that can render tanks as well as any other armored vehicles useless. Because of this installation, the skids have had to be redesigned to have a greater height.

If it is necessary, housings can be located on the lateral mounts for medium, heavy or multi-barrel machine-guns, 68mm SNEB or 81mm SNORA rocket launchers, infrared self-defence missiles or other arms systems that may be required by different users. Other requirements have been satisfied by various installations, such as a powerful searchlight on the forward underside of the fuselage, the positioning of flotation bags on the skids for emergency sea landings or two stretchers to evacuate wounded. These can allow emergency take offs with up to 10 people on board.

TECHNICAL CHARACTERISTICS BO-105-CB

COST:	6 million dollars		Maximum load	500 kg
DIMENSIONS:			**Internal fuel capacity**	**570 l**
Length	11.86 m		**PROPULSION:**	
Height	3.02 m		Two Allison 250-C20B jet engines with a total thrust	
Main rotor diameter	9.84 m		of 840 HP	
Tail rotor diameter	1.90 m		**PERFORMANCE:**	
Main rotor turning area	76.05 m²		Service ceiling height	3,050 m
WEIGHT:			Maximum speed	242 km/h
Empty	1,277 kg		Range	596 km
Maximum	**2,500 kg**			

Widely tested in combat, the Gazelle light helicopter combines great agility with the possibility of employing a wide range of arms systems. These aspects give it its capacity to take part in all-weather attack missions against armor plated targets, and different types of aircraft.

MULTI-PURPOSE

Originally designed as a model capable of carrying out multiple tasks, the SA-342 has shown itself to be suitable for liaison missions, anti-tank actions, all types of support, helicopter hunting, VIP transport, evacuations, air medical support, reconnaissance, and more.

The Middle East, the Falklands, the Gulf War and Yugoslavia have been war settings where it has participated in the fulfilment of combat missions, reconnaissance, transport or evacuation. With its small size and operational possibilities, it is a model with varied capabilities, although its low level of self-protection makes it very vulnerable against modern battlefield threats.

Programme

Conceived as X-300 by the French company Sud Aviation, to replace the Alouette II, the first prototype of a light machine with a capacity for five occupants, designated SA 340, made its first flight on the 7th of April 1967. It was propelled by a 360 HP Astazou II jet engine. That year, a joint-production agreement was reached with the British company Westland Helicopters, and exactly one year later, a second model flew.

ACTIVE

In spite of the years that have passed since its design, the Gazelle is a very operational model, which will remain in service with front-line units until about 2010.

Development stages

After solving initial problems with the four-blade rotor configuration, four redesigned SA341 pre-production models were ordered, which were destined for a complete operational evaluation. Sud Aviation was taken over by Aerospatiale, coinciding with the arrival of production orders, and the first model corresponding to the series flew on the 6th of April 1971. Some changes had been introduced, such as an enlarged cockpit, semi-articulated rotors and an increase in the maximum take-off weight to 1,800 kg.

The model went into service with the French (ALAT) and British (RAF) air forces

HELICOPTER HUNTER

The latest update of the Gazelle allows it to act as a helicopter hunter, thanks to the integration of the Matra ATAM system which allows it to fire self-guided air to air Mistral missiles, a fact which increases its action potential in all phases of combat.

RELOADING

The weaponry can easily be replaced by the crew taking advantage of areas logistically established, which increase the mission capability when faced with multiple threats.

in 1973. These machines were later modernised to different standards depending on the missions they had to carry out.

Since May 1983 a version has been produced with higher engine performance, increasing the take-off capacity by 100kg. It was designated SA342 in its French military model, SA342K for export and SA342L for the model incorporating tail rotor modifications. Furthermore, the SA342L came out in 1985 with a maximum weight of 2000kg.

Users

More than a thousand of these helicopters, in their military and civil versions, have been bought by a total of 32 countries which use them as much for traffic surveillance as for anti-helicopter missions. Standing out among the military operators are; Ecuador with 13 units, Egypt with 80, some of which were assembled under licence; France with 340 of various versions; Iraq, with 50, widely used in the war with Iran; Yugoslavia, with 200 constructed under licence, Libya with 40, whose maintenance must suffer due to the international embargo; Morocco with 30 distributed between the Air Force and the police, Great Britain with 200, and Syria with 55, some of which were captured by the Israelis who have used them to support their own

missions. To the above must be added countries like Angola, Burundi, Cameroon, China, Croatia, Cyprus, Gabon, Ireland, Kenya, Kuwait, Lebanon, Malawi, Qatar, Senegal, Trinidad, and Tobago, Tunisia and the United Arab Emirates.

In Combat

During Britain's deployment of forces to recapture the Falkland Islands, a total of 17 AH.Mk1 machines were assigned to the Royal Marines. They carried out armed reconnaissance activities, with 68mm Matra SNEB rocket launchers and a machine gun on the side of the cockpit. Three of them were shot down by the Argentineans, which showed evidence of their lack of robustness for combat.

In 1980 the Iraqis employed their Gazelles, armed with HOT anti-tank missiles and GIAT 20mm cannons, against Iranian troops, during the first Gulf war. Meanwhile,

FENESTRON

The tail structure includes a small tailplane, tail fairing and a thirteen blade rotor integrated into a circular structure within the tail which increases the safety of use in any action zone.

SPECIALIZED

A new observation and guidance assembly and four HOT anti-tank missiles characterice the tank-hunting model of the Gazelle that is in service with the French army.

during the 1982 invasion of Lebanon, the Israelis shot down and captured various Syrian units. The French and British deployed their reconnaissance and anti-tank squadrons to stop the threat from Iraqi troops who had invaded Kuwait in 1991. The Moroccans have used theirs against the Frente Polisario, and some machines have been heavily used during the peace-keeping operations in the former Yugoslavia, where they have served in liaison, VIP transport and support missions.

TECHNICAL CHARACTERISTICS: SA-342 GAZELLE

COST:	6 million dollars		Maximum external load	700 kg
DIMENSIONS:			Fuel	445 l
Length	11.97 m		**PROPULSION:**	One Turbomeca Astazou XIV jet engine with 890 HP thrust
Height	3.18 m			
Main rotor length	10.50 m		**FEATURES:**	
Main rotor turning area	86.50 m²		Service ceiling height	4,300 m
WEIGHT:			Maximum speed	310 km/h
Empty	917 kg		Ascent speed	8.5 m/s
Maximum	1,900 kg		Maximum range	755 km

Design

With some advanced features for the period in which it was conceived, the Gazelle was designed fulfilling some very satisfactory requirements with respect to its combat capability, associated arms systems, reliability of use, ease of maintenance and reduced operation costs.

Structure

Made up of various interconnected elements, the fuselage consists of the cabin structure based on a light alloy framework that supports the windows and doors. The central section is made up of honeycombed

PROPULSION

Immediately below the main rotor head, which turns the three blades, is the gear cooling system. Behind this is the small Astazou Turbomeca propulsion unit that incorporates an air intake with a filter, covered by a red fabric, and an exhaust, pointing upwards.

tail fairing.

The floor is made up of panels of different materials in laminated layers and there are two wide steel-tube skids on which wheels can be situated to ease its movement on hard surfaces. Of some note here, is its semi-articulated rotor, which turns a laminated fibre three blad-ed main propeller and a tail rotor located inside a casing known as a FENESTRON to carry out the necessary operations. In front of the tail rotor are two large tailplanes that give it the lateral stability necessary to facilitate all its movements.

panels that constitute the passenger area, and the fuel tanks, it also supports the gearbox. The rear section, on top of which is the propulsion unit, serves to support the transmission axle that passes through its upper part and gives rigidity to the

Propulsion

Located in a position far enough back with respect to the main rotor is the jet engine. With an air intake incorporating a particle separator screen or a filter, the engine is an axial Turbomeca Astazou IIIA

are fixings on both sides of the fuselage in which housings for 68mm rocket launchers or 2.75" HOT or TOW guided anti-tank missiles can be installed. These reach their objectives thanks to the use of gyro stabilized viewfinders located in the upper part of the cockpit. In the case of the specialized French units, the SFIM APX397, weaponry consists of medium machine guns and light cannons, with the 20mm GIAT M261. Lately anti-helicopter and anti-ship versions have been undergoing evaluation, incorporating Mistral Matra light missile launchers provided with passive infra-red trackers which guide the missiles to their target, while many units have received interference flare launchers to make it more difficult to be shot down by active or

turbo-axle. With a power output of 590HP in its original version and 890HP in the improved version , which the SA 342's use, it integrates an exhaust tube that directs the exhaust gases upwards, thanks to the current generated by the movement of the main rotor. This decreases the infra-red signature that would have made it very easy to shoot down with anti-aircraft missiles equipped with heat-seeking heads.

The configuration

The pilot and co-pilot fly together in the cockpit in their indivudual seats enjoying what is a very good view of the outside world thanks to the large windowed section in front of them. Behind them, in the back of the cockpit there is an additional seating area containing a bench with standard equipment including seatbelts and a further capacity to hold up to three more people if the necessity demands it. The result is a helicopter which offers further expansion possibilities and therefore the potential for a variety of activities.

The weaponry installed depends on the mission to be carried out, however there

passive search missiles.

When it is necessary the helicpter can be used as a lightweight transporter for a variety of different uses, being fitted with a hook on the underside of the fuselage which by attaching a sling to the cargo is capable of holding and moving weights of up to 700 kg. The helicopter also has a special winch which is very useful and fundamental to many kinds of rescue operations, being capable of hoisting loads of up to 135 kg. in a variety of conditions.

S pecifically designed to be used as an armed helicopter during the Vietnam War, the AH-1 COBRA and its updated version SUPER COBRA have demonstrated great versatility and high potential. This has motivated the creation of improved versions that it is thought will remain in service until the end of the second decade of the 21st century.

Very agile and maneuverable, with the incorporation of a main rotor with only two blades, it has been widely used in the conflicts in Vietnam, Lebanon, Grenada, Panama and the Gulf War. In missions in these conflicts its robustness and potential as a combat unit were well demonstrated, despite

OPTIMIZED

Although the AH-1 has been in service for many years, the modern Cobra family includes optimized versions that have been fully updated to conform with the elements of modern combat.

CANNON

There is a General Electric GTK4A/A assembly installed underneath the front part of the fuselage which includes a three-barrelled M197 gun mounting with three 20mm cannons, capable of firing limited bursts of 16 rounds at a maximum rate of 675 rounds per minute.

---

some having been shot down for being more vulnerable than other more modern designs which incorporate better physical and electronic self-defence elements.

The need is created

It was first produced in June 1962, the fruit of a private corporate development, known as the D-255 Iroquois Warrior. It also incorporated some elements developed for the Bell UH-1 Utility Helicopter. The requirements of the United States Army for the AAFSS program (Advanced Aerial Fire Support System) necessitated its development into a concept known as Model 209, the prototype of which flew on the 7th of September 1965.

The selection of model 209

This was selected on the 7th of April 1966, when two test models were contracted, that were followed six days later by 110 production machines; the first AH-1G's were sent to Vietnam in August 1967. The mission needs in this conflict, in which several hundred of these machines were

Air Squadron of the Spanish Navy, followed by advanced models such as CONFICS, ALLD, ATAFCS or SMASH, depending on the tracking systems installed.

The former was followed by the AH-1Q with the capacity for launching TOW missiles; the AH-1S with more powerful engines that increase its agility and maneuverability; the AH-1P with flat walls on the sides of the cockpit and warning radar; the AH-1E with 20mm cannon M197 mountings and the AH-1F, optimized for anti-tank combat.

The United States Marines have also acquired twin-engine models designated "Super Cobra", which include the models AH-1J and AH-1T, modified in order to gain more maneuverability and improve its

shot down or suffered accidents, prompted the Marine Corps to adopt the machine in a better designed twin-engine model, designated the AH-1J Super Cobra, that was ready in 1969.

The introduction of new capabilities, such as the launching of TOW anti-tank guided missiles, the incorporation of more powerful engines, its provision with improved avionics and other small details have led to the construction of two thousand machines. These have also been acquired by other nations, among which are Israel, Turkey, Greece, Iran, Jordan, Pakistan, Spain, Bahrain, South Korea, Thailand, and under licence in Rumania and Japan.

chances in air to air combat. There is also the AH-1W which corresponds to the most powerful version currently in service and which has now been programmed to be modernised up to the standard AH-1W/4BW models. These incorporate General Electric T700-GE-4101 jet engines with infrared suppressers, new avionics, a high-resolution FLIR tracker, improved stub wings, and more. These transformed models are set to be handed over to the forces between 2004 and 2013.

The Cobra family

The large range of Cobra helicopters produced includes a long evolution of models adapted to the necessities of the moment. The first prototype of Model 209 incorporates a retractable undercarriage on the underside of the fuselage that was substituted by a fixed unit with two skids on the production models. The first model to enter service was the AH-1G, of which 8 models were destined for the 7th Armed

The Super Cobra

Designed by the USMC and bought by Turkey and Romania, the AH-1W "Super Cobra" is the most powerful model of the Cobra family designed to date. It stands out as much for the survival possibilities the two engines give it, as for the high agility derived from the employment of a two-bladed propeller for the main rotor.

Characteristic

With a similar fuselage in all the models of the range, this helicopter presents a notably narrow profile that makes its

EMBARKING

The Marine Corps which travel in the amphibious assault ships of the United States Marines normally include half a dozen Cobra attack helicopters among their allocated equipment.

upper part is the main rotor which moves a large double-bladed propeller and which is driven by two General Electric T700-GE-401 jet engines, capable of generating a combined power of 3,250HP. They are provided with a large cover, which facilitates maintenance tasks. The rear section is elongated and includes the small tail rotor with a 2.94m diameter propeller which has been manufactured in combined aluminium and steel.

To optimize the work of the crew, and their capability to face the missions entrusted to them, there is a Kaiser Data Display for

detection from the front difficult and reduces its radar and infrared signature. The cockpit is the tandem type with the pilot seated in the rear section, raised-up to obtain better visibility of what is happening outside, and the co-pilot systems operator located in the front part, from where he uses the viewfinder that allows aiming and firing. Both incorporate displays compatible with use of night goggles, and have lateral and underside protection against light-arm impact, and enjoy air conditioning.

The central area of the front section incorporates two skids on the lower part that allow landing on any surface. On the

the pilot, AN/APN-194 altimeter radar, AN/APN-44(V) radar warner, AN/ALE-39 interference flare launchers, Teledyne AN/APN-21 navigation radar based on Doppler impulses with Collins display screens, and coded communication links.

Potential

The inclusion of an M65 viewfinder, modified with an NTSF-65 thermal imaging camera from the Israeli Company Rafael, give it the capacity for daytime and night time operations and for the use of advanced weaponry. Notable amongst these are the GTK4A/A General Electric nose turret

which includes a three-barrelled M197 gun-mounting with three 20mm cannons of 1.52 meter length that are capable of firing limited bursts of 16 rounds at a rate of 675 rounds per minute. Their feed drum is capable of housing 750 rounds. The firing angle is 220° side-to-side, 50° downwards and 18° upwards.

On the side stub wings 70mm rocket launchers can be positioned that range from the LAU-69As with 7 tubes, to the LAU-61As with 19 tubes CBU-55B housings of air-combustible explosives; SUU-44/A flare-

MAINTENANCE

Conceived for combat, the Cobra requires specialist maintenance to tune up the multiple systems that give it its capacity for attack missions.

MISSIONS

Identified by the initials SFOR on the fuselage, these Cobras have carried out armed reconnaissance missions over the former-Yugoslav skies during the peacekeeping phase assigned to NATO.

launchers, M118 grenade-launchers, GPU-2A or SUU-11A/A containers for 7.62x51mm multi-barrelled Minigun machine-guns, TOW or AGM-114 "Hellfire" anti-tank missiles, Hughes AGM-65D "Maverik" surface-attack missiles, or air to air AIM-9L "Sidewinder" missiles. A very wide range of weapons that give it enough power to take part in escort missions, armed reconnaissance, target identification or attack against mechanized or armored vehicles.

In combat

With respect to the use of arms it has been demonstrated that the Israeli AH-1Ss have used the "Hellfire" missiles to attack the buildings of the headquarters of the fundamentalist Hezbollah group and the Palestinian positions in the south of Lebanon. Meanwhile the United States machines had the highest operational readiness of all the helicopters that took part in the operations to free Kuwait. One operation that particularly stands out was the neutralization of the first armored units of a column of 1000 vehicles on a bridge, using TOW missiles. Once immobilized they were easy prey for the rest of the weapons used by the international coalition force.

TECHNICAL CHARACTERISTICS AH-1W

COST:	10.7 million dollars		Maximum load arms and fuel:	2,019 kg
DIMENSIONS:			**Internal fuel**	1,128 l
Length	13.87 m		**PROPULSION:**	TWO GENERAL ELECTRIC T700-GE-401 JET ENGINES,
Height	4.11 m			EACH UNIT WITH A POWER OF 1,625 HP
Rotor diameter	14.63 m		**PERFORMANCE:**	
Rotor turning area	168.11 m²		Service ceiling height	4,495 m
WEIGHT:			**Maximum speed**	352 km/h
Empty	4,671 kg		Cruising speed	278 km/h
Maximum	6,690 kg		Range	587 km

CO-PILOT

The gunner/bombardier co-pilot has for his use a view-finder connected to the front tracking turret. He is in charge of firing the arms systems with the side lever, which includes a red-colored trigger.

SENSORS

A stabilized housing contains the navigation and guidance sensors of the AH-1, consisting of a thermal imaging camera, television camera, laser rangefinder equipment and so on. These components allow it to operate equally well by day as by night, and in adverse weather conditions.

CANNONS

The M197 mounting incorporates three 20mm cannons that can fire bursts of up to 3,000 rounds per minute and enjoys a wide angle of fire in order to confront land-based or aerial targets.

ROTOR

Developed from that of the Bell UH-1 helicopter, the principal rotor head is articulated, turns clockwise and has shown itself suitable to give the Cobra a high level of flight agility.

TWIN JET ENGINES

The Super Cobra version of the Marines includes 2 General Electric T700-GE-401 jet engines that produce a total of 3,250HP, with which the helicopter can perform its combat missions without restriction equally over open sea or land.

TAIL

The rotor is incorporated in the upper part of the tail structure, which has the function of maintaining directional stability. There are right-angle section stabilizers on the sides and a skid underneath that protect the tail beam against possible blows during take-off or landing.

STUB WINGS

Each of the two stub wings consists of two rigid fixings for TOW anti-tank missiles, rocket launchers, incendiary liquid tanks, a variety of missiles, transport containers and other systems. Recently, a magazine has been installed on top of the wings for launching interference flares.

SKIDS

Underneath the main structure are the two skids, one on each side, that allow the machine to operate from any surface and have shown great durability throughout its service. To facilitate movement on the ground, a pair of small wheels can be fixed to the front parts.

The need of European armies and their associated industries to carry out a series of significant actions created the concept of the Eurocopter Attack Helicopter-Tiger, which is presented as an advanced response within the growing field of specialized machines created to meet the current demand.

Versatile, capable, powerful and, above all, European. This helicopter has been developed thanks to the combined efforts of France and Germany, by reaching self-sufficient production neither ruled out that other countries like Sweden, Spain, and Australia (were the PT4 prototype crashed during trials in February 1998) will end up going for this model to replace the existing air-fleet dedicated to attack and anti-tank missions.

LAUNCHES
Acceptance trials have allowed the integration of the ATAM Matra system in the "Tiger" so that it can deploy MISTRAL air to air missiles to attack other helicopters or aeroplanes in flight at high or low altitude, and its possibilities for combat missions are significantly increasing.

CAPABILITY
We can see a STINGER air to air missile being fired by one of the prototypes configured in accordance with the German request for a multipurpose attack helicopter capable of different types of missions.

Conception

The planned program to substitute, during the 1990's, the attack helicopters the "Gazelle" and Bo-105, in service in France and Germany respectively, brought the governments of both countries to an agreement to develop an anti-tank helicopter. The first contacts were made in 1984 and on the 13th of November 1987 a firm decision was made; the development contract was signed on the 30th of November 1989 by the Eurocopter company formed by the French Aerospatiale and German Messerschmit Bölkow Blohm (MBB) companies.

The Evaluations

The initial forecast was for the construction of three unarmed prototypes for aerodynamic evaluation. One configured for tank-hunting, designated "Gerfaut", and another completed to carry out mixtures of attack and reconnaissance missions, reaching a climax with the flight of the PTI on the 27th of April 1991, from which construction continued until the completion of five helicopters on the 21st of February 1997.

As well as static and vibration trials, inspection of fuselages, verification of equipment integration etc, diverse flight trials have been executed which include the launching of HOT-2 missiles by the PT-5 in May 1997 up to the validation of its ability to

operate in Arctic conditions, for which the PT4 carried out exercises in Sweden equipped with skids below the wheels to land and take off in snow covered land at -30°C.

Supplies

Although the constant reductions in the defence budgets of European countries participating in the program have influenced the quantity of equipment produced, and the period foreseen for entering service. The signing up for production phase, on the 30th of June 1995, gave impetus for the programmed introduction into service in the first few years of the 21st century.

In addition the PT4 has already fired its

PROTOTYPES

Five prototype units are being used to validate the features of the "Tiger", which it is hoped will go into production in the first few years of the 21st century.

Deployment possibilities

Although the "Tiger" is immersed in the development and pre-production phase, it is demonstrating that its deployment possibilities and mission capabilities are as were hoped. It is a design which incorporates the latest advanced technology to take it into multiple types of missions.

Advanced characteristics

Conceived using the most advanced technology such as a structure which is made up of 80% composite materials without rivets, titanium, aluminium, Kevlar etc which gives it the capacity to withstand collisions with the ground of up to 10.5

front cannon and launched MISTRAL air-to-air missiles and non-guided rockets, in response to the HAP French support and escort validation requirements. Meanwhile, the PT5 has launched the STINGER air-to-air missile, corresponding with the UHT/HAC multi-purpose combat and support version. The French foresee incorporating the 115 HAP and 100 HAC, while the Germans have asked for the 212 UHT. A delivery process will begin in 2001 that could last up to halfway through the second decade of the 21st century, that is, if the estimated number of units to be supplied is not reduced.

meters per second, and equipped with two MTU/Rolls Royce/Turbomeca MTR390 jet engines which each produce 1,285 horsepower and 1,558 in times of emergency. With exhaust nozzles integrated in the fuselage to reduce its signature, the TIGER is an attack machine born to neutralize present and future threats in every type of environment and situation. The four-bladed main rotor is constructed combining elastomeric fibres and composite materials which have an indefinite life-span, the landing gear is fixed and permits landings of up to 6 meters per second, and there are redundant hydraulic, electrical and fuel supply systems

The cockpit

The cockpit has been configured to minimize the crew's work. Manufactured in a tandem design with the pilot positioned at the front and the gunner in the back, the cockpit incorporates the latest avionic advances with multifunctional color presentation screens, control display units (CDU), automatic flight control systems (AFCS), intercommunication systems (ICS), radio frequency indicators (RFI), alarm display screen, and weapon control panels. The pilot and gunner can use helmets with protection visors onto which can be projected a variety of flight data and parameters and which also have an integrated holographic system to facilitate weapon-firing. This has elements to facilitate communication between the different data parts or with systems which are on the same side. Self defence is assigned to the Thomson -CSF TSC2000 system with an IFF friend -enemy interrogator, communication and laser-threat alarm, and interference systems launcher.

Capability

The TIGER has been configured as a multipurpose helicopter, based on a modular concept, with the possibility of being equipped with various systems which allow it maximum operational flexibility and to be able to assume new roles whenever necessary; as well as adapting itself to the continuous changes in international politics.

The HAP variant includes television and infra-red sensors, FLIR (Forward Looking Infrared), for nocturnal flights, measuring distances by lasers with optical elements to capture and follow targets. These are installed in a giro-stabilized housing SFIM/TRT STRIX positioned behind the upper part of the pilot's cockpit. Its weaponry consists of an automatic cannon GIAT M-78 positioned below the nose, provided with up to 450 thirty millimeter rounds, while on the wings there are two fixing points where 12 or 24 rockets (68mm SNEB) can be positioned. The machine is also equipped with armor piercing darts and four MISTRAL air-to-air-missiles.

The UHT/HAC includes a mast above the rotor which supports the OSIRIS Euromep Sensor conceived from a second generation targeting system which includes FLIR, laser and TV, while below the nose a FLIR is integrated for the purpose of flying.

Its weaponry consists of rocket-launchers, heavy machine gun batteries or light

HAP

The French version HAP is a new generation combat helicopter with air-to-air and ground support capacity, for which it has a 30mm cannon in the turret, 68mm rocket launchers and MATRA MISTRAL air-to-air missiles which make it a difficult adversary in combat.

cannons. STINGER air-to-air missiles will be fitted to the machines ordered by Germany and anti-tank missiles in the HOT-2 and TRIGAT versions.

Up to four of these can be positioned on each wing, the first guided by the SACLOS system and the second being of the fire and forget type. The HOT-2 has been validated in trials carried out between May and June in 1997, in one of which shooting was done with the helicopter flying backwards at a speed of 140 km/hour, while to homogenize the TRIGAT it is fired at by a PANTHER helicopter, with modifications incorporated in the TIGER from 1998.

TIGER

This French-German combat helicopter can carry out its missions at night, in bad weather and is capable of carrying a wide range of weaponry which enable it to manage a variety of threats and defensive missions.

Conceived by the Soviet industry as a technological reply to the United States Apache, the Mi-24 was created to complement the powerful Hind. It comes from a long tradition of manufacturing by the company Mil which has built an excess of 31,000 helicopters. The continual lack of funds has impeded its construction of large runs and its construction has depended on different sources. Seventy units are in active service with the Russian Federation Air Force.

Creating a need

Despite the fact that the Soviets had exported a lot of the Hind Helicopters to many of its orbital countries (political and economical) the continual advances introduced by western countries, with designs

MULTIPLE

Its robustness, weaponry capacity and armor-plating make the Mi-28 capable of multiple missions in every kind of battlefield and in the most adverse meteorological conditions.

like the Italian Mangusta, the United States Cobra and Apache, made Russian strategists decide to create a new model which would include everything a modern attack helicopter needed. This was to be supplied to their own armed forces in a way which would also act as a possible export channel.

Development

Taking as a reference the project carried out by Alexei Ivanov, the initial design work began in 1980 in the Mil OKB Factory. The first of the four prototypes had its first flight on the 10th of November 1982. In the 1989 Bourget Airshow the third of these was presented to the western public having just completed 90% of the development process after 800 hours of flight. Produced by Rost-vertol in Rostov, its introduction was very slow and export orders were not arriving,

although it was being evaluated in Sweden. Despite this, from January 1994 it was being worked on to meet the requirements of the Mi-28N concept; which is capable of operating at night and in bad weather. This was the reason for the radar mounted above the rotor which could be seen in the last part of the Bourget Paris Airshow.

Different versions

The initial forecast was to construct up to six different versions of which the anti-tank series would occupy the greater part of the production capacity. It would also be used to replace the oldest HIND models. The basis of the development would allow the evolution of a model with greater capacity to operate in any weather, satisfying the needs of a variety of nations interested in robust, capable Russian designs.

Another version being worked on is for the navy, with protection systems to work in this kind of environment. Designed to operate from amphibious vessels giving marines cover when they are disembarking and, at the same time, being able to confront threats such as patrol boats.

Finally, let's describe the capabilities of specific versions optimized for air-to-air combat with other similar helicopters and with the ability to face aeroplanes in slow and low flights and others designed for anti-missile purposes.

HAVOC

With a low rate of production due to the continual reduction in the Russian defence budget, the Mi-28 is a machine conceived to replace other older models which are out of step with newer western models.

CANON

Integrated at the front and below the fuselage, the 30mm cannon is fed by two ammunition magazines and is capable of controlled bursts of fire of up to 900 rounds per minute with an effective reach of more than two kilometres against surface or air targets.

Missions Types

Although the philosophy for the deployment of helicopters in Russia has gone through changes after some experimentation, it is being used at division level in ground units where it is favored for its quick utilization and deployment through an effective chain of command.

Missions trusted to the helicopter would involve tasks such as close support offensives, attacks against armored formations, eliminating enemy anti-aircraft defences, anti-helicopter defences, rearguard operations and general support. It operates together with fixed-wing planes such as the Su-25 "Frogfoot" and its variants.

These tasks are carried out in three zones. The first is a band of 15 kilometres depth inside enemy lines and in this area it carries out anti-tank missions and neutralization of missile and electronic defence systems. The second extends up to 30 km and in this area supports the operations of its own side's airplanes; meanwhile the third covers up to 150 km and includes deep penetrations to accompany infiltration helicopters and rescue missions for pilots who have been shot down.

A design with special features

With a very similar design in much of its conception to its western equivalents, the United States Defence Department declared that in principal the HAVOC was a copy of the APACHE. However this machine presents a variety of interesting peculiarities as a result of the different conceptions of the industry which produced it and which was looking to combine robustness with its other features.

The structure

It is robust and heavily-armored, the cockpit includes mechanical flight controls moved with hydraulic assistance and the latest development sees the installation of liquid crystal display screens (LCDs). From the cockpit to the main rotor which has five blades receiving rotary power from two Kimov TV3-117VM Jet Engines which produce 2,070 horsepower each. They are located in lateral gondolas with infra-red suppressers in the outlets that the signature is 2.5 times less than its predecessor the Mi-24. Between both Gondolas is a small Ivcheknko AI-9V Jet Engine which acts as an auxiliary power unit to start up the propulsion units if they need external assistance.

The fuel tanks which supply the propulsion units have a capacity of 1,665 litres and are filled with a polyurethane foam designed to avoid accidental explosions. In its interior it is covered with a layer of latex which seals holes produced by projectiles or shrapnel.

POWER

A radar fitted above the main rotor, a complex radio guidance system located in the front section, launchers at the extremes of the wings where the weaponry is located, a 30mm cannon at the front, and a long list of etceteras for this powerful Russian attack machine.

At the height of the entrance nozzles for the turbines we find the components which make up the main landing carriage which are notable for their high-capacity for absorbing the shocks of impacts up to 17 meters per second.

A design for survival

Designed for the highest level of survival, the cockpit and main features of this

Capability

Usually, flying at altitudes less than 20 meters avoids neutralization, and this machine incorporates in its front section a complex monitoring and flight support system which includes a small radar transmitter for guiding missiles, an image intensifying television camera, a laser transmitter and soon it will incorporate a FLIR infra-red tracking system.

These advanced and extremely effective components, which are connected to

machine are heavily armour plated against every type of light arms attack with components of titanium and composite materials specifically designed for such use. The cockpit seats have a pyrotechnic system which tenses the harnesses in the event of impacts and are provided with parachutes in case of emergency. Positioned in these seats the pilots enjoy the protection of a cockpit which resists 20mm impacts and flat glass windows which are designed to cope with 12.7mm projectiles. The whole front part resists light arms fire from distances of 30 meters.

The fixed-landing carriage is very robust and the cockpit floor employs panels which follow the bee-hive model giving it the capability of surviving a vertical fall of up to 17 meters per second without any of the crew coming to any harm.

its own navigation system, give it the possibility of employing its own weaponry in a way which is able to give it a much greater guarantee of success. The 30 mm 2A42 cannon is mounted in the turret which can be found just below the nose at the front of the helicopter, and is fed by two magazines with a capacity of 250 rounds. In addition there are two fixtures for more weapons located below the stub wings which can be used to hold infra-red rocket launchers. These mounts are capable of carrying up to 480 kilograms of arms.

A standard configuration for this helicopter could be considered as one which includes 16 AT-6 Spiral Anti-Tank missiles, or instead could involve using the new Ataka System. This is a launcher where the missiles have a maximum range of 8 kilometers, or an effective range of 5 km, and when non-guided up to 80 km. Yet another alternative is to use 122 mm rocket-launchers for what is a different kind of mission, in air-to-air combat whith other enemy aircraft.

HAVOC MI-28 TECHNICAL CHARACTERISTICS

COST IN MILLIONS OF DOLLARS:	Unknown		Internal fuel	1,665 kg
DIMENSIONS:			**PROPULSION:**	
Length, excluding rotors	17.01 m		Two Klimov TV3-117VM jet engines capable of producing together 4,140 horsepower	
Height	4.70 m			
Wingspan	4.88 m		**PERFORMANCE:**	
Diameter of main rotor	17.20 m		Service ceiling height	5,800 m
Main rotor turning area	232.35 m²		Maximum speed	300 km/h
WEIGHT:			Tactical operational range	200 km
Empty	8,095 kg		Reach	1,100 km
Maximum	11,660 kg		Design factor	+3/-0,5 g's

COCKPIT

The glass covering the cockpit of the pilot and co-pilot/gunner is designed to avoid revealing reflections and is thick enough to absorb the impact of weapons up to 12.7mm caliber.

SENSORS

Radar for guiding missiles, laser rangefinder and an infra-red tracking module are some of the sensors integrated in the front part of the Mi-28 which give it a high-altitude flight position in the launching of its diverse weapons package.

LANDING CARRIAGE

The major elements of the landing carriage incorporate a shock absorption system which cushions the fuselage in ground impacts up to a velocity of 17 meters per second and without which the crew would be injured.

ROTOR

The radar ,installed in a housing above the main 5-bladed rotor, has improved the possibility of employing the aircraft in whatever kind of meteorological conditions.

TAIL

The tail part has a 4-bladed rotor which improves directional stability and also has a small wheel which, in this area, softens impacts against the ground on landing.

STUB WINGS

The stub wings support the weapon load with, at their extremities, housings which launch interference flares and underneath there are two robust supports, one incorporating 8 ATAKA anti-tank missiles and the other twenty 80mm rockets.

FUSELAGE

Incorporated in the upper part of the fuselage are enemy tranmission detectors and communication aerials and it is highlighted that additional equipment or personnel can be carried in this area.

Following the opening up process of other ex-Soviet companies, KAMOV has been incorporated into the military and industrial company Mapo. It has recently been promoting two new attack helicopters which comply with the requirements demanded of aircraft which have to confront the threats of the 21st century.

The first known as Ka -50 Hokum-A, is a single-seater attack machine characterised by its compact size and some notable features. While the second, the Ka-52 Hokum-B, is an older, re-equipped single-seater version. To help with their exportation, they have been christened the Black Shark and Alligator respectively.

EVALUATION

With the fuselage painted in desert tones more in step with use in the Middle East, the various BLACK SHARK prototypes are being consciously evaluated with a view to their possible adoption as a standard attack helicopter in a variety of countries.

CAPABILITY

With its design, special features, and multi-purpose weaponry, the Ka-50 stands out from other models currently being offered in the world market.

The origins

Helicopters like the Ka-27, Ka-29, Ka31RLD and Ka-32 took up a large part of the purchases of the Soviet Navy. After which the company KAMOV worked on the design of an attack machine which would satisfy the requirements of the Russian Army and which was conceptually similar to the HAVOC with which it competed inside and outside the Russian market.

Conception

After initial studies the design of the Ka-50 project was ready at the end of 1977 and work began on the manufacture of the the first prototype, initially known as V-80Sh I (VERTOLYET-80). This flew for the first time on the 27th of July 1982, its existence became known in the summer of 1984, when the first photographs of it were published in the 1989 report "Soviet Military Power", published by the United States Defense Department. Western specialists were able to observe and get to know it during the 1992 Farnborough Air Festival where it was called the Werewolf, a name substituted later on by the existing one.

Development

The objective was to have 12 pre-production

units manufactured at the Arsenyev factory, two of which were moved in 1995 to the Russian Army's aviation training center in Torzhok. During which time work continued on the verification and implementation of this single-seater attack machine. Known as the Alligator, with the code name V-80ash2, it was presented at Le Bourget Festival in 1995 and flew in 1996. Incorporating some advanced electronic equipment from France in those units destined for export. It can be deployed as a transitional, operational, or training machine for pilots heading for combat units.

Evaluations

Its adoption has been considered by some countries including Slovakia which negotiated the purchase of six single-seaters to equip an air force squadron. The objective of Sergei Mikheyev, a doctor of

technical sciences and chief designer of the company Kamov, is that some of his two attack helicopters will be adopted by the Russian Armed Forces.

Capability

Although the Russian models are manifestly technically inferior to their western equivalents, their robustness, reliability, low purchase price, low running cost and capability as multi-purpose machines make them attractive in a variety of markets.

The design

Following the line in the positioning and type of propulsion used by previous models of this design company, the new KAMOVS are characterized by being the first single-seater helicopters in the world specializing in attack missions. With a thinner fuselage in the single-seater and more rounded one in the twin-seater these models are highlighted by the positioning of a large part of the flight sensors and target detectors in the front nose and a ball with additional sensors positioned above the cockpit for future versions.

Heavily armored- it is estimated that 750 kg of material has been used- the structure has been constructed around a torsion box principle which includes various apertures with access panels for internal equipment

and as such improves access for maintenance work. It stands out for its weaponry, retractable landing carriage, and it is provided with low pressure wheels to allow it to operate on any type of terrain. There are two large stabilizers located in the upper part of the helicopter and in the tail there is a directional rudder instead of a rotor.

SINGLE-SEATER

The Ka-52 is a single-seater model, optimized from the original design, which incorporates various improvements in its tracking and guidance weapon systems. Of these there is a ball containing various systems which is particularly noticeable, located above the cockpit.

Propulsion

Two KLIMOV jet engines TV3-117KV with a thrust of 2,190 horsepower each drive the single-seater and an earlier version has been modified to increase the power up to 2,465 horsepower to drive the two-seater craft. They are positioned on the upper parts of the sides of the fuse-

The pilot or pilots, depending on the model, are located in a strongly protected cockpit provided with armored glass which protects them from direct impacts of up to 23mm fired from 100m, and at the same time includes a unique evacuation system, called the ZVEZDA K-37, which consists of an activator which explodes the rotors and fires a rocket to sweep the crew towards the outside where they can then use their parachutes to land safe and sound. The associated flight equipment includes ground tracking radar, HUD data screen similar to the MIG-29, VHF, UHF and HF communication systems, friend-enemy detector, ground map displays etc.

DISPLAY

The display screen in the pilot's cockpit offers the possibility of observing possible targets, to facilitate the guidance of weapon systems. The concept highlights the somewhat antiquated nature of the design when compared with those of western countries.

lage to prevent anti-aircraft fire from hitting both of them at the same time. The entrance nozzles have spherical deflectors positioned in front of them to make it difficult for foreign bodies to enter and the

TECHNICAL CHARACTERISTICS

	Ka-50	Ka-52	PROPULSION:		
COST IN MILLIONS OF DOLLARS:	Unknown	Unknown		2 KLIMOV V3-T117VK Jet engines with a total thurust of 4,380 horsepower	2 KLIMOV V3-T117VMA Jet engines with a total thurust of 4,930 horsepower
DIMENSIONS:					
Length	16 m	13.53 m (fuselage)			
Height	4,93 m	4.95 m			
Rotor diameter	14,5 m	14.5 m	PERFORMANCE:		
Surface area each rotor	165,13 m²	165.13 m²	Stationary celling	4.000 m	3.600 m
WEIGHT:			Maximum speed	350 km/h	300 km/h
Operational	9.800 kg	10,400 kg	Ascent capability	600 m/s	480 m/s
Maximum external load	2.000 kg	2,000 kg	Combat operational range	250 km	200 km
External fuel load	2.000 l	2,000 l	Design factor	+ 3 g's	+ 3 g's

exhaust nozzles are designed to offer the lowest possible infra-red signature.

Power is transmitted through a gearbox to the counter rotation double rotor system, which has three blades each. Each of these rotors has been been designed to resist light impacts and can be dismantled for transportation in the hold of cargo aircraft like the Il-76. This kind of configuration makes a tail rotor unnecessary and dispenses with the sophisticated and vulnerable transmission systems that run through the upper part of the fuselage to transmit power from the propulsion unit. A small jet engine can be found on the upper central part of the fuselage which acts as an auxiliary power source to allow the starting up of the KLAMOV and which also supplies electric and hydraulic power for support work on the ground.

In combat

Identical weapon systems can be found in both of the models, these being associated with the active and passive avionics sys-

WEAPONRY

Two robust supports under the wings allow the fixing of different combinations of weaponry, up to a maximum weight of around three tonnes. Anti-tank laser guided missiles are used to neutralize armor plated vehicles.

tems incorporated on board the aircraft. These give the helicopters the capability of detecting and finding their objectives over very long distances, during the day or night, or even in the most adverse of weather conditions.

The helicopter's powerful 30 mm 2A42 cannon assembly can be found on the left side of the fuselage. This assembly is maneuverable because of a hydraulic system which allows the cannon's position to be changed by up to 30 degrees vertically and then 6 degrees laterally, and which is fed by two magazines located in the center of the fuselage. These magazines have the capacity to hold 460 rounds of either armor-piercing or high-powered explosive shells. The stub wings are positioned on the sides of the fuselage in such a way that they almost appear to be truly functioning wings, but which instead allow the loading

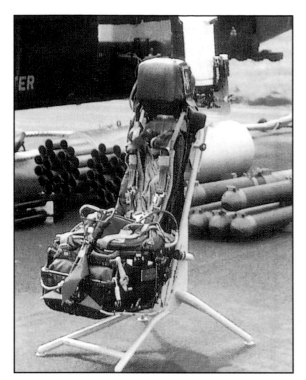

DESIGN
Conceived with a double rotor as in other KAMOV designs the KA-50 is notable for its compact size, the philosophy of use and mission capability in all types of atmospheric conditions (photograph on the right).

of a wide variety of weapon combinations able to reach a total of some two tones in weight. Launchers are positioned at the extremities of the stub wings with a capacity for holding up to 128 flares. These perfom the function of a self-defence system, acting as decoys against enemy missiles tracking the helicopter and its thermal signature.

There are also two further positions where the following variety of equipment can be installed: AT-X-16 Vikhr anti-tank modules with the capability of holding up to 6 laser guided missiles with a range of some 10 kilometers; non-guided B8V20A rocket-launchers which can hold up to twenty S-8 rockets; the B-13 rocket launcher with a total of five S-13 rockets; the UPK-23-250 housings which are used to hold two 23 mm cannons; 250 and 500 kilogram free-fall bombs; KMGU submunitions launchers; large 500 litre fuel tanks and Igla-V air-to-air missiles. It has the capability of carrying and then launching Hegler AS-12 anti-radiation missiles and Aphid AA-8 and Archer AA-11 air-to-air missiles. This capability has been highlighted because it gives this helicopter the possibility of engaging a variety of different kinds of enemy fighter bombers and attack aircraft in combat.

ARMOUR
The KA-50 fuselage structure has been strongly armored to resist impacts from medium caliber weapons which allows it to operate without restrictions in the front line (photograph below).

Widely used to transport troops and equipment during the Vietnam War, as well as limited support and attack missions. The different versions of the UH-1 demonstrated their suitability to meet the requirements that a truly lightweight multi-purpose helicopter must be capable of. Although many of them were lost in combat, their mission capabili-

MANOEUVRES
The Spanish Army's Airborne Forces (FAMET) include various battalions of helicopters equipped with the UH-1H which has demonstrated its robustness and effectiveness to meet any kind of transport or support mission working with ground forces.

ties, ease of maintenance, reduced purchase price and mulit-purpose operational and capability characteristics have had a bearing on the fact that they can still be found in service in a variety of armies around the world where it is seen as the ideal solution to carry out the most varied of missions.

Conception

The requirements of the United States Army was to have a multi-purpose helicopter which could serve to evacuate the injured from the front line, an experience greatly felt during the Korean War with the transportation from mobile MASH units to hospitals. This led the BELL Company to come up with a proposal, known as MODEL 204 which ended up as the army's choice during the course of 1955.

Development

After the first flight of the XH-40 which took place on the 22nd of October in 1956. A rapid period of trials began which led to

MULTI-PURPOSE
The design and features of the IROQUOIS has meant that it has established itself in the world at large as a multi-purpose machine which is notable for its low purchase and operational cost.

the order to construct half a dozen YH-40's with the objective of an even greater and ambitious program of appraisal.

The following nine UH-1 helicopters incorporated changes to the original design such as a jet engine with 860 horsepower and canvas seats to transport six people.

Popularly known as HUEY, a name which the manufacturer engraved on the craft's command controls, the supply of the first UH-1A's began on the 30th of June 1959, and were completed in March 1961. later they received the nicknames, SLICK for the troop

carrier, HOG for the gunship version and IROQUOIS for the multi-purpose H model. The A model machines were the first to be sent to Vietnam as a part of the Tactical Transportation Company which arrived at Saigon airport in Tan Son Nhut at the beginning of 1963 to facilitate troop deployment.

Evolution

The UH-1B version began being delivered in 1961 and included a more powerful engine of 960 horsepower and greater load and personnel capacity. From this point many others followed , more optimized and with improved features such as the 767 examples of the C model which had a greater fuel capacity, wider blades and a tail rotor with an inverted

profile. The 2,201 machines of the D model which were propelled by a 1,100 horsepower jet engine and with a capacity to take 12 soldiers, 360 units of which were constructed under licence by the German company Dornier. The E model with modifications to allow it to operate from the amphibious assault craft; the F model supplied with a 1,272 horsepower engine and used by the United States Airforce to support the siting of the Minuteman and Titan ballistic missile silos of the Strategic Air Command. The F model with 5,345 machines manufactured for the United States Army, with the LYCOMING T53-L-13 engine of 1,400 horsepower and elongated fuselage to facilitate the movement of greater loads and personnel.

A great diffusion

This last version is the most popular one which has survived up to the present day with many modifications to the instrument panels, to allow the use of night goggles, for example, and with the installment of new equipment such as radio altimeters, radar emission detectors and supplementary armor for the pilot seats. The D and H series have been given the reference of BELL 205.

The various models have been identified by a base letter preceding the designation. As such, the letter T is assigned for missions of engagement, E for electronic warfare, H for rescue, R for reconnaissance etc. Twin engined versions have also been manufactured such as the UH-1N and AB-212, depending on whether the construction was carried out in the United States or in Italy, and whether it is four-bladed or not as in the BELL 412.

In service

Manufactured in various configurations in factories in the United States, Italy, Germany, Japan, Indonesia and Canada, the different versions of the ubiquitous UH-1 have exceeded 10,000 units, amongst which are 100 BN models (Blade November) requested by the United States Marine Corps from Bell Helicopter Texetron, and to be ready by the end of the year 2003.

In service with the armed forces of more than seventy countries, amongst those are: The United States, Saudi Arabia, Argentina, Bahrein, Brunei, The Czech Republic, Ecuador, Slovenia, Finland, Greece, Guatemala, The Netherlands, Honduras, Israel, Italy, Japan, Morocco, Mexico, Thailand, Turkey, Uruguay and Venezuela. In Spain there are some seventy examples of the H and 212 versions, carrying out active service in the army and navy and they make

ACTIVE SERVICE
Despite the introduction of the more modern UH-60 a total of 1,300 craft continue forming a part of the helicopter wing of the United States Army, which continues to obtain notable results which are derived from its design, mission possibilities, performance and low maintenance work.

EMBARKATION
With twin jet engines and up to date equipment, the hundred UH-1N helicopters used by the marine corps have been modernized to prolong their useful lives.

SUPPORT
To give support fire for its own troops the «H» series can be equipped with multiple machine guns, rocket-launchers, grenade-launchers etc. These give the helicopter an additional combat capacity for all types of missions and support tasks.

up the main element of the Helicopter Battalion (BHELMA) and the Third Air Squadron respectively.

The design philosophy

The BELL 204/205 family of helicopters are designed with a broad cross-section hull, constructed in light alloy and, with the exception of the 412, incorporate a semi-rigid rotor consisting of two articulated blades which determine the plane of rotation by means of a stabilizer.

An innovative helicopter

Huey was the first helicopter of the series which used a jet engine, a LYCOMING T53, installed above the fuselage and close to the main rotor unit, just behind the gearbox unit. This allowed a larger cargo hold and ability to transport more. The

UH-1H TECHNICAL CHARACTERISTICS

COST:	5 million dollars		Internal fuel	945 l
DIMENSIONS:			PROPULSION:	A Lycoming T53-L-13 jet engine with a thrust of 1,400 horsepower
Length	13,59 m			
Height	4,41 m		PERFORMANCE:	
Rotor diameter	14,63 m		Service ceiling height	3.840 m
Main rotor turning area	168,1 m²		Maximum height	240 km/h
WEIGHT:			Range flying at ground level	512 km
Empty	2.363 kg		Range with auxilliary tanks and	
Maximum	4.309 kg		flying at 1,120m altitude	800 km
Max external load	2.000 kg			

design maintained in its different versions the use of the most powerful and reliable twin motors for flying with the least risk over areas like the sea.

The pilot and co-pilot are together in the cockpit and have access to the interior through side doors, enjoying good visibility to the outside world thanks to large glass windows. The passenger or transport area is accessed by the large sliding doors on the

PILOTS

Sat in seats protected against impacts and provided with helmets which facilitate communications, the IROQUOIS pilot and co-pilot of BHELMA II have the responsibility to operate this aircraft when making night flights for commando infiltration missions.

TWIN-MOTOR

The UH-1N has been given a double turbine which increases its survival possibilities in case of the failure of one of the engines, a basic requirement when it is being operated continually above the sea surface.

side of the craft. This area is where the flight mechanic works and carries out auxiliary tasks. The design is notable for its tail beam inclined upwards with rectangular stabilizers in the central part and a small rotor at the end. It has two skids which make it possible to land in any of terrain.

The normal capacity of the H model makes it possible to transport a dozen fully- equipped soldiers in reconfigurable canvas seats, or depending on need, there could be stretchers or two tons cargo in the hold. Using a sling system it can also carry light vehicles or medium caliber artillery pieces which are hung from a hook inside the helicopter.

In combat

This helicopter was extensively used in the Vietnam War from 1963 onwards and there are many photographs and images

which were widely seen in war films being shown around the world. These images are an accurate representation of the huge of variety of missions performed by this aircraft. These covered activities such as medical air evacuations: the trasportation and collection of troops at different enemy infiltration positions; air patrols of river routes; reconnaisance work; the support of artillery fire and assaults; inteligence work; psychological warfare; giving support fire for ground troops; the combined use of medium, heavy and multi-barrelled machine guns; rocket and grenade launching etc.

Subsequently and in addition to various peace-keeping missions with the UN, models of this helicopter have carried out operations extensively in conflicts such as the Arab-Israeli War, the invasion of Grenada, the peacekeeping operation in Iraqi Kurdistan, the former Yugoslavia, and in operation Desert Storm. During which marine helicopters were used to designate targets at night, thanks to systems such as Nite Eagle which, has an infra-red tracker and laser direction signaler.

Weaponry

The UH-1's weapons can be used with great versatility, such as machine guns used with the cargo hold's access doors open, like the modern MK-2 Marte anti-ship mis-

MODERNIZATION

The BELL 412 is a modernized version of the original design which includes a double turbine, structural improvements and up-dated cockpit and is outstanding as a support element in transport missions.

CAPABILITY

Equipped with two 12.7x99mm heavy machine guns, grenade launchers and rocket launchers the UH-1H is prepared to give punctual and powerful replies to attack actions.

siles which are carried by the Italian **Griffon** helicopters, a design version which has evolved from the Bell 412.

Basically the different versions of these helicopters can have a variety of weapons fitted in the cargo area as well as externally on the aircraft's fuselage. These are options which depend on the type of missions envisioned for them, but in each case the control of the weapons can be carried out by the operators sitting at the front of the cockpit.

The mounts fitted to the inside of the helicopter are straightforward constructions allowing the operation of both the SACO M-60 medium machine gun and the Browning M-2HB heavy machine gun. There are also automatic 40 mm grenade-launching systems and multiple machine gun assemblies such as the MINIGUN, which has a rate of fire of 6000 rounds per minute.

The experience of the Vietnam conflict consolidated the use of helicopters for support work during all phases of combat, this included material transportation as well as support for troops on the ground. As in previous experiences, the introduction of the Black Hawk family as a utilitarian machine adapted to modern requirements was the driving force for a wide range of different versions, created to satisfy the most varied of needs.

Requirements

In 1972, after analysing the requirements for the new helicopter established in the study UTTAS (Utility Tactical Aircraft System), the United States Army requested companies to present their proposals to develop the aircraft needed.

Decision

Boeing Vertol and Sikorsky Aircraft were

PROVEN

With the years gone by since its entry into service, the number of units constructed and the conflicts in which it has been used, the design formula of the BLACK HAWK has been validated. It has demonstrated that it was able to carry out all foreseeable missions and that it has great capability to grow with new possibilities of use.

NUMEROUS

Close to a thousand and a half BLACK HAWKS make up the transport helicopter arsenal of the United States Armed Forces to which can be added those units exported to some twenty countries.

MULTI-PURPOSE

Employed in transport or light attack missions, the BLACK HAWK has demonstrated itself to be a multi-purpose machine which can be adapted, after the inclusion of the necessary equipment, to carry out all kinds of missions.

selected and on the 30th of August 1972 they were each contracted to construct three prototypes which were extensively tested between 1974 and 1975. The YUH-60 flew for the first time on the 17th of October 1974.

It was necessary to construct a fourth

machine for trials, financed by the manufacturing companies, to complete evaluations which lasted up to November 1976. On the 23rd of December 1976 the YUH-60A was declared the winner which was confirmed by the first order for 15 units.

Called the UH-60A Black Hawk in 1979, the first units were sent to the 101st Air Transport Division of Fort Campbell in Kentucky. From this point a production rate of 10 units per month was reached. This has been

continued up to the present as there are more than two thousand of these helicopters in service around the world.

Existing Models

The initial version, the UH-60A has been designed to carry three crew members and eleven fully-equipped soldiers. It can be used without any modifications to perform tasks such as medical evacuations, recon-

ARMED

Although it wasn't designed to carry out armed missions the inclusions of two wings allows it to support a variety of weapons from rocket launchers to Hellfire anti-tank missiles, with which it can support ground troops or act as a light attack craft.

is used by the United States Air force to rescue pilots shot down. The SH-60 SEAHAWK is designed for submarine hunting and surface attacks. The AH-60L is used to support direct penetrations with various types of weaponry. The VH-60 is used to transport VIP's (Very Important People) including the President of the United Estates. The UH-60Q DUSTOFF for naval medical evacuation and the CH-60 for general use. This version

naissance, management and control, logistics support, and mine dispersing with the VOLCANO System. This is thanks to some modifications which allow quick and easy changes in configuration. The basic model has been improved since 1989 and its designation has been changed to UH-60L.

The EH-60 is more specialized with the electronic war system QUICK FIX IIB and later modifications, JUH-60A and GUH-60A were used for trials and technical evaluation. The MH-60 is also equipped with weaponry and systems necessary to carry out special operations. The HH/MG-60G PAVE HAWK

has been evaluated by the U.S. Navy since the 6 th. of october 1977. With the result that the company has received firm orders for these machines until 2001.

ADVANCED

Designed according to some wide reaching requirements the UH-60 has demonstrated itself to be one of the most advanced helicopters of its kind in service at the moment.

The users

To those previously mentioned would have to be added the S-70 version for export. Amongst others the Saudi Arabian contract is notable twelve S-70A-1 Desert Hawks with the capacity to transport 15 soldiers with the aid of extra fuel tanks. Sixteen S-70A-IL for medical evacuations with six stretchers, infra-red search lights and improved communication equipment. Two S-70A-5 units employed by the Philippine Airforce. Thirty nine S-70A-9 units assigned to the Australian Airforce, two of which crashed recently when they were transporting SAS commandos. Three S-70A-11 to Jordan. Two S-70A-15 VIP transporters acquired by Brunei. Twelve S-70A-17 used by the Turkish Army and Police, which have been complemented by with fifty more manufactured under licence by TAI. Two S-70A-21 VIP units used in Egypt. Three S-70A-22 VIP used in Korea and others bought by Mexico, The Moroccan Police, Hong Kong and Argentine Armed Forces.

The direct transfers of United States units include the UH-60L's sent to Bahrain, five requested for by Brunei, fourteen UH-60A & L used to combat the Colombian

MEDEVAC

This medical evacuation craft has a cargo hold for four stretchers and a medical team with the possibility of increasing its range of action by optimizing the sub-wing fuel tanks.

narcotics trade. Ten UH-60A YANSHUF assigned to the Israeli 124 Squadron and twelve of the same model lent to the U.S. Drug Enforcement Agency, which monitors the introduction of narcotics and sixteen type L's for Kuwait. As well as these are those units designated S-70A-16, applicable for those produced under licence by the British company GNK Westland. Also to be added are the hundred machines constructed by the Japanese company Mitsubishi since 1988. These correspond to the models SH-60J Jayhawk for search and rescue and the UH-60J for general purpose.

Design characteristics

Widely proven in combat the Black Hawk has demonstrated that its design characteristics allow it to successfully deal with the requirements of a modern battlefield. Noteworthy for its robustness, ease of maintenance and capability to carry out multiple missions.

A resistant machine

During the invasion of the island of Grenada in 1983, some of these machines were attacked by light arms and demonstrated that a fuselage with a combination of tita-

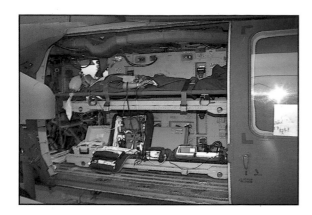

nium, Kevlar, graphite, and plastic fibres was capable of resisting the impacts. It has a fixed landing carriage with pneumatic shock-absorbers incorporated in both front wheels to lessen the blow in the event of heavy falls to the ground. Trials have demonstrated that 85% of the structure remains intact after suffering vertical impacts of 11.5m/s, lateral of 9.1 meters per second and longitudinal of 12.2.

At the same time, projectiles of 23mm diameter can pass through the main and tail rotor blades without causing serious damage; the 1,361 liter fuel tanks are resistant to impacts and include anti-explosion elements; the electrical and hydraulic systems are duplicated; the pilots can count on armored plating protectors on the side walls and below their seats and the cargo deck floor has been reinforced to check light arm fire.

Configuration

Since 1989 it has incorporated two General Electric T700-GE-701C Jet Engines which together generate a thrust of 3,600 horsepower and are connected to the titanium main rotor which includes four blades of 8 meters length, complemented by a small tail rotor positioned at an angle to the vertical.

The pilot and co-pilot sit in the control cockpit which has been designed with instrumentation compatible with night vision goggles. They have at their disposition different flight elements including a double hydraulic system for managing the blade angle, the AFCS Hamilton digital auto-pilot, self-stabilization equipment, the Omega AN/ARN-148 Tracor navigator, Motorola AN/LST-5B satellite communications UHF etc.

Defined as a machine designed by the military for the military, this helicopter represents a landmark in United States industry, and has reached a high level of safety and operational capacity in every combat operation in which it has been employed. A notable feature is its ability to fold the wings and tail rotor for transportation in specific types of planes such as the C-130 HERCULES where there is enough space in the cargo hold for one helicopter, or the C-5 GALAXY which can fit up to five.

Capacity

Designed as a multi-purpose helicopter for multiple missions, the UH-60 is basically a light transport machine which, for example, can carry two infantry platoons or a 105mm artillery piece hooked up on a sling underneath it, with the gunners and ammunition inside.

For self-defence it incorporates passive electronic systems and interference flare launchers in the upper part of the fuselage. At the same time there are anchoring points at the side windows from where the third crew member can operate a medium

or heavy machine gun. In addition the more modern models can have side wings added where auxiliary fuel tanks rocket launchers, Minigun multiple barrel machine guns or up to 16 third generation Hellfire anti-tank missiles can also be added. These require a ground laser or light helicopter such as the Kiowa OH-58 with a laser to guide the missile to the target.

SUPPORT

The third crew member has the responsibility for operating the gun mounting installed in the windows behind the cockpit which is used with medium or heavy machine guns such as the 7.62x51mm SACO M60 or 12.7x99mm BROWNING M-2B HB respectively. Low recoil cannons have also been experimented with.

ROTOR

The main rotor is basically made of titanium and has the job of moving four large blades which give the helicopter the stability and manoeuvrability necessary for its operational missions.

COCKPIT

The pilot and co-pilot cockpit includes all the necessary elements to allow the helicopter to fly night and day in any atmospheric conditions.

UH-60L TECHNICAL CHARACTERISTICS

COST:	5,87 million dollars		**Internal fuel load**	1,361 l
DIMENSIONS:			**Maximum fuel load**	6,507 l
Fuselage length	15.26 m		**PROPULSION:**	Two General Electric T700-GE-701C jet engines with a thrust of 1,800 horsepower each.
Height	5.13 m			
Length with rotor turning	19.76 m		**PERFORMANCE:**	
Cockpit volume	11.61 m³		Service ceiling height	5,837 m
Rotor turning area	8.68 m²		Maximum speed	361 km/h
WEIGHT:			Cruising speed	294 km/h
Empty	5,224 kg		Stationary maximum height	2,895 m
Maximum	11,113 kg		Range	584 km
Internal max load	1,197 kg		Extended range	2,222 km
External max load	3,629 kg			

STUB WINGS

Defined as an external load hook-up system, modern models include the possibility of connecting auxiliary fuel tanks or a wide range of weapon systems.

PROPULSION

Accessed by two large sliding doors, the two General Electric T700-GE-701C Jet Engines are located above the transport hold and give the necessary agility for missions entrusted to this helicopter. They are fitted with large outlet nozzles which have special units installed to reduce the infra-red emissions.

FLARE LAUNCHERS

Incorporated on the fuselage sides are M-130 interference flare launchers which serve the purpose of confusing infra-red seeking missiles and also those guided by radar.

CARRIAGE

The front landing carriage incorporates a pneumatic shock absorption system to which has been added a cable cutting system, and which allows the absorption of impacts up to 11.5 meters per second to reduce the effect of the personnel transporter making an emergency landing.

FUSELAGE

The back part of the fuselage incorporates a small warning light for position, the tactical communication system aerials and a small wheel designed to be able to cope with the vigorous landings which are possible when used in combat.

Widely used as assault craft from the amphibious boats of the United States Navy. The CH-46 has demonstrated for more than thirty years of service its capacity to perform all types of transport activities, especially those related with troops and materials of the United States Marine Corps.

Vietnam, Lebanon, Grenada, Kuwait, Somalia, Liberia, and Albania, among others, are some of the areas of the world where they have been deployed to carry out combat actions, evaluation missions or support tasks for multinational deployments.

Origins

In 1956, the firm Vertol began design and engineering studies in order to develop a twin-jet engine transport helicopter that might have military and commercial applications, and which could use the small and light jet engines which were then starting to be available in the aeronautic market.

Development

After validating the concept in the prototype model 107, which flew for the first time on the 22nd of April 1958, orders arrived for three evaluation models of a military version known as CH-46A, for the United States Army. They would later abandon its incorporation in favor of the larger and more powerful CH-47 Chinook. After

---

IN COMBAT

Deployed within the SFOR unit sent by NATO to the former Yugoslavia, the CH-46E have performed continuous logistical transport missions as much from their mother ships as from final bases.

MAINTENANCE

The years have passed since its entry into service, and its continual use on all types of missions has required a constant maintenance process in order to maintain the machines at the highest operational level.

---

nine machines had been purchased by New York Airways, the representatives of the United States Marine Corps saw in this machine the answer to their needs for a large capacity advanced twin-engine model for troop transport during amphibious assault operations.

Acquisition

In February 1961, fourteen CH-46A machines were ordered by the marines. The first of which flew on the 16th of October 1962. Later US Navy evaluations followed. They aquired fifty UH-46s during 1964 for logistical transport operations. In 1965, the Japanese firm Kawasaki received the authorization to construct the helicopter under license and at the same time the United States Defence Ministry ordered the doubling of the production rate in order to satisfy the needs of the Vietnam conflict. Because of this, at the start of the seventies, 164 model A, and 266 model D machines had been built.

To the former followed 186 model F units delivered from 1968 on with additional electronic equipment. There were also some E models manufactured from 1977. They were based on previous versions in which more powerful engines were installed and modifications to the pilot's seats were made in order to reduce the impact in case of falls to the ground. Also, the HH-46D and RH-46 were employed respectively on rescue and mine-hunting missions on behalf of the Navy; the KV-107II/IIA was constructed under licence in Japan, of which 17 were exported to Saudi Arabia. To these we must include the CH-113 "Labrador", acquired by

the Canadian Air Force to carry out SAR missions, the CH-113A "Voyager" which were delivered to the Canadian Army between 1964 and 1965, and the 55 Kkp 4C constructed for the Swedish Navy and Air Force. Of these last units, 45 were assigned to submarine and mine-hunting operations.

Improvements

Called "Frog" by its crew, almost 300 CH-46E Sea Knights are currently still in service. The majority of them are used by the Marines in 16 active and 2 reserve squadrons. To these can be added the twenty machines used for crew training. Their current operational availability is due to the various improvement processes that have been applied to the original machines, such as the CILOP carried out during the seventies in order to replace the rotor blades with lighter and stronger fiber-glass ones. Also, a more powerful propulsion unit was added and structural reinforcements made that increased its survival capabilities in case of

capacity substantially increased.

Additionally, defense systems have been installed such as flare launchers and electronic countermeasure equipment. Paint with a better infrared signature has replaced the original, and some areas have been reinforced with armor plating. The cockpit now includes warning radar connected to an infra-red generator to confuse first generation ground-air missiles. The instrument panels have now been adapted for the use of night goggles and some machines have been equipped with the Communications Navigation Cockpit System (CNCS) which includes digital radios, navigation equipment and a global positioning system (GPS). For its part, the Navy is introducing to its machines a Dynamic Component Upgrade (DUC), which has been contracted with Boeing Defense and Space since 1995.

accident or during combat missions. Meanwhile, at the end of the eighties, the Service Life Extension Program (SLEP) and Helicopter Emergency Flotation System (HEFS) meant improvements were introduced, with the latter to increase its emergency landing resistance capability, having had the fuel tank

Design

Compact and capable, the CH-46 suffers from some limiting features inherent to the age of its design. Although throughout its years of service, it has shown its durability and efficiency to fulfil its assigned activities.

of the amphibious ships that normally transport them. This is also useful when maintenance tasks need to be carried out.

Tactics

During the Vietnam era, when it flew at high altitude to avoid being hit by light anti-aircraft fire. The machine nowadays carries out missions such as Terrain Flight Missions (TERF) in which the machine flies at an altitude of between 15 and 20 meters or less, in order to take advantage of the ruggedness of the terrain and to make it difficult to locate. Assaults *en masse* combine the advantage of surprise with the difficulty of enemy reaction against multiple targets. The capabilities of the crew are put to the test in The Nap of the Earth Flight (NOE), in which it flies at an altitude of less than 15 meters along previously studied routes. They are also challenged in the Combined Arms exercises (CAX) which are carried out in the Californian desert zone of Twenty-nine Palms. In both operations, on board personnel are in charge of operating through two side windows two 12.70 x 99mm Browning M-2 heavy machine guns that constitute its defencive and support armaments.

Structure

This is the result of a fuselage manufactured in aluminum alloy, designed in order to achieve the greatest interior space and access for cargo and personnel. In its upper part are the reinforcements that support the transmission and the propulsion unit. Entry is through a rear access ramp and in the interior situated on the sides, there are two rows of seating. There is capacity for up to twenty-six fully-equipped soldiers, or to transport all types of combat support equipment, from light missile-launchers to munitions and logistical support. It can also be adapted for medical evacuations with fifteen stretchers and two medics. A hook situated on the underside allows a crane to winch up cargoes of 4,535 kilograms.

ROBUST

After thirty years unbroken service, the "Sea Knight" design has shown itself to be very robust and adaptable to the basic needs of capacity and weight required by the United States Marines, which plans to replace the current fleet before the year 2010.

Propulsion

Two powerful and reliable General Electric T58-GE-16 Jet Engines, improvements on the original version, each rendering a maximum of 1,870 horsepower, give it the necessary power to complete the assigned missions, and be able to return to base with only one engine working.

These engines turn two large three-blade rotors in tandem, one in the front part and the other in the rear section. They turn in opposite directions to improve stability during stationary flight. Their blades can be retracted rapidly through a system controlled from the cockpit. This greatly facilitates the storage capacity on deck or in the hangars

COCKPIT

Provided with a large glass windscreen which favors visibility, and equipped with radar emission detectors on the outside. The cockpit has been configured with simple and operational analogue equipment.

STERN

On each of the sides of the rear section, a half-gondola is located housing the rear undercarriage components, different types of electronic equipment including anti-skid panels on the upper part to facilitate maintenance tasks in this area of the fuselage.

PROPULSION

Incorporated in the upper rear part of the fuselage, just below the tail rotor, are the two General Electric T58-GE-16 Jet Engines propulsion units that produce a total thrust of 3,470HP with which the agility and capacity of this medium-type helicopter is guaranteed.

ARMED

A small window on each side allows the siting of a medium and heavy machine gun for self-defense tasks, easily carried out when the window is removed. For this there is a mounting permitting exact lateral and vertical movements of the weapon.

DETAIL

The complexity of the cabling and fluid pipes integrated into the fuselage are obvious in this shot taken from the right-hand side door, which includes an access ladder to facilitate the entry and exit of the crew.

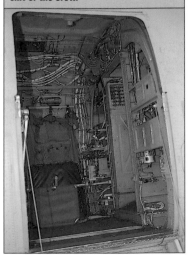

ROTORS

The rotors, which include a triple-bladed head, can be retracted automatically and correspond to a very effective although outdated design. They are ideal for transport missions that involve low and medium altitude flight.

EQUIPMENT

The forward hold, in the helicopter nose, houses a large part of the electronic equipment and systems associated with the cockpit instrumentation and contains the components necessary to ensure safe flight over the sea and in any weather conditions.

FRONT UNDERCARRIAGE

Robust, with pneumatic shock absorbers to reduce the impact on the two steerable wheels, the front undercarriage is characterized by its simplicity and small size.

TECHNICAL CHARACTERISTICS CH-46E

COST:	16 million dollars	Maximum internal cargo	4,000 kg
DIMENSIONS:		Internal fuel	3,786 l
Length	13.66 m	ROPULSION:	
Height	5.09 m	Two General Electric T58-GE-16 jet engines units producing a total thrust of 3,740 HP	
Rotor diameters	15.24 m		
Rotor surface area	364.6 m²	FEATURES:	
Hold area	16.72 m²	Service ceiling	4,265 m
WEIGHT:		Maximum velocity	267 km/h
Empty	5,927 kg	Range	383 km
Maximum	10,433 kg		

Considered as one of the most powerful of western helicopters, the Chinook, is distinguished from the rest by its capability to transport all types of cargo. Widely tested in combat, from Vietnam to the Falklands, it has demonstrated its robustness and range of use in many situations. The Chinook is able to carry a large number of troops, and carry large items of equipment by using the fixed points under the fuselage.

Development

As a reply to a United States Army

OPERATION

With its features, possibilities and performance, the CH-47D "Chinook" is one of the most capable transport helicopters, for this reason more than a thousand have been manufactured and are now in service in about twenty countries across the world.

OPERATIONAL

Various CH-47D's have been operating within NATO's forces assigned to the transportation of soldiers, weapons, and materials of every kind.

requirement issued in 1957 for the supply of a heavy helicopter VERTOL, which merged with Boeing in 1960, offered its CH-46 design which was considered to be insufficient. Because of this, the bigger V-114 was created with greater endurance designed for the US Army first as the YHC-1B in 1962, and then later as the CH-47 "Chinook".

Evolution

A YHC-1B prototype was revealed for the first time on the 21st of September 1961 and was quickly put through a process of validation along with four others. This culminated in a formal request for the helicopter to go into production. The CH-47 was propelled by LYCOMING T55-L-5 jet engines with 2,200 horsepower each and with a capability of moving 2,790 kilograms over a distance of 111 miles, or 6,068 kg over a distance of 22 miles.

The first units were received on the 16th of August 1962 by the First Airborne Cavalry Division which would use a large part of the 354 units produced of this version.

On the 10th of May 1967 the CH-47B was introduced with more powerful 2,850 horsepower jet engines, of which 108 machines were manufactured. On the 14th of October in the same year the CH47-C flew which led to the delivery of 270 units, each with 3,750 horsepower T55-L-11A engines. In 1973 a modernization process began on 182 CH-47 units with the introduction of new rotor blades manufactured with composite materials. Using faster inspection methods and in 1976, the process of reconfiguring the CH-47D began with the oldest models.

After the flight of the prototype in 1979, a production program was began which resulted in deliveries in February 1984 to the 101 Air Transport Division. After which 470 units of the new CH-47D were requested and delivered up to 1994 to the United States Army, which wants to keep them in active service until 2025, by which time its replacement, currently known as the AAN is due to be in service. Other modernization programs, such as the I.H.C. are also under consideration at present.

Specialisation

Special versions such as the MH-47D used by The Special Operations Command Regiment have come out of the original design. These following on from the AH-47 GUNSHIP version of the Vietnam era. They are capable of being re-supplied in flight and are equipped with thermal imaginy cameras, BENDIX/KING RDR -1300 meteorological radars, two 7.62 MINIGUN mul-

> **THE UNITED STATES**
> The United States ground forces operate with around five hundred CHINOOKS to support both normal and special missions with another two hundred being used by the National Guard.

> **SPAIN**
> The airforce units of the Spanish Army (FAMET) employ seventeen CH-47 units in the Helicopter Transport Battalion (BHELTRA) around the Madrid area.

tiple barrel machine gun assemblies, radar warners, electronic war equipment, ELBIT ANVIS-7 night vision goggles and a hoist winch with a capacity of 272kg. The machine also has the capability of transporting 44 soldiers. In addition there are the GCH-47 models which have been configured for engineering training work and the Mk2 of the British Royal Air Force updated to a Mk3 version for the special forces.

Exports

Of the thousands of units manufactured by Boeing; 10 have gone to civilian companies, 5 to Argentina where three operate in the army and two with the airforce, 12 to Australia, 9 to Canada, 2 to Japan, 6 to the Netherlands, 6 to Singapore, 24 to South Korea, 19 to Spain which lost two in accidents and where the rest are assigned to the Helicopter Transport Battalion (BHELTRA), 3 to Taiwan, 6 to Thailand, 58 to Great Britain, and 734 to the United States of which 540 have been modernized.

A production license has been given to the Japanese company KAWASAKI which is manufacturing 56 machines, of which 40 are for the country's army and 16 for the airforce. The Italian company AGUSTA has produced 134 machines, destined for Egypt, Greece, Iran, Italy, Libya, Morocco and the Pennsylvanian National Air Guard which has received 11 units manufactured in Italy.

Characteristics

The design which led to its considerable size and cargo capacity are characteristics very much appreciated by the those in the military who work with this model.

Fuselage

It has a constant metallic cross-section, very wide and elongated, with five small observation windows along the side. If also has a large door at the back which allows the rapid disembarkation of troops or material, even when hovering over uneven terrain. A side door on the front right part of the fuselage and an advanced cockpit with lateral windows allow the pilots to escape in times of emergency.

The need to carry out flights in any weather condition has meant that the latest model includes every kind of advanced display to help the pilots including: radar altimeter, automatic stabilization, VOR receiver, TACAN, complex HF & UHF communication equipment, horizontal position indicator, satellite links, global positioners etc. The cockpit has been modified to allow it to carry out night flights using night vision goggles without any compatibility problems with the instruments. For daytime flights visibility is very good with the large front window and with two additional crew members who have responsibility for observation at the large rear door and side windows to facilitate the work of the pilots.

The fuselage sides are prominent with the front section containing the electronic systems and the rest incorporating fuel tanks, which have a capacity of 3,899 liters, and associated equipment. On the underside

TECHNICAL CHARACTERISTICS

COST:	30 million dollars		Maximum load	12,284 kg
DIMENSION:			**Internal fuel**	3,902 l
Length	30.14 m		**PROPULSION:**	
Height	5.78 m			Two Allied Signal T-55-L-714 turbines with a joint thrust
Rotor diameter	18.29 m			of 8,336 horsepower
Rotor turning area	525.3 m²		**PERFORMANCE:**	
WEIGHT:			Service ceiling height	3,095 m
Empty	10,693 kg		Maximum speed	298 km/h
Maximum	24,494 kg		Range of action	185 km

there are the four fixed landing carriage units, the front two with two wheels each and pneumatic shock-absorbers, the back two with one wheel each which can be orientated.

Propulsion

Two Allied Signal T55-L-712 SBB jet engines are located externally in two lateral gondolas on the large tail rotor structure, each with a maximum of 4,314 horse-power. The 714 model has an increased power of 4,867 horsepower in times of emergency. Two very large rotors, each made up of three blades, turn at 225 revolutions per minute, coupled to a gearbox which can cope with power loadings of up to 7,500 horsepower. These blades are constructed in such a way that they have a honeycombed nucleus, covered with glass fibre laminate which can resist impacts of up to 20mm. The rear rotor is positioned significantly higher than the front one.

The engines, which have proven themselves to be very robust and which have a low incidence of break-downs, are fed by fixed fuel tanks on the fuselage and by other auxiliary tanks with a capacity of

CAPABILITY

The ramp at the rear allows fast embarking and disembarking of troops and material, while the hook-up fixings below the fuselage permit the transportation of all kinds of cargo like these two 105mm Oto Malera light artillery guns with their ammunition and equipment.

COCKPIT

The pilot and co-pilot enjoy a cockpit designed in a rational manner, equipped with all the necessary instrumentation to facilitate their flight and transport operations.

9,084 litres located in the cargo hold. The APU Solar T62-T-2B auxiliary power unit drives a 20kVA generator and hydraulic pumping system which produces the necessary electrical and hydraulic power, independent of external support.

Capacity

The large size of the hold, with a surface area of 21 square meters and volume of 41 cubic meters, permits it to be configured for a variety of different kinds of personnel transport thanks to the seats which are strategically incorporated along the sides in a manner allowing space for 44

the 155mm M198 gun which is hung from a sling, while the gunners and associated equipment including ammunition are transported inside the helicopter.

Self-defence is trusted to a radar emission detector, interference flare-launchers and when necessary two 12.7mm Browning M-2HB medium machine guns can be installed at the door and window behind the cockpit. These are operated by the two additional crew members, who make up a total crew on board of four people. The British models have TRACOR chaff-launchers, HONEYWELL AN/AAR-47 alarm systems for the approach of missiles, LORAL AN/ALQ-157 and GEC-MARCONI AR118228 RWR infra-red interference systems. This is equipment derived from its extensive use in real combat missions.

fully-equipped soldiers, this can be increased to 55 in times of emergency.

The large size of the rear door allows the embarkation of light vehicles, pneuma-

tic equipment, artillery guns, missile systems etc. It also allows for the fast disembarkation of parachutists in either the traditional manual or automatic way. In the bottom part of the fuselage are hooks for hoisting cargo, the central one with a capacity of 11,793 kg and the other two 7,711 kg. The combination of these allow the quick movement of heavy artillery pieces such as

Created to satisfy heavy transport needs, the CH-53 has consolidated itself as the helicopter with the greatest capacity for carrying cargo designed and, in service in the West at the moment. Its features and possibilities have been brought out in various battle missions,

HEAVY DUTY
With its capacity and features the CH-53E SUPER STALLION can be considered capable of transporting more men and cargo than any other machine in service in the Western armed forces. It has also demonstrated itself as a great multipurpose helicopter in those countries which have equipped themselves with it.

from operation CSAR to rescue Captain O'Grady, a United States F-16 pilot shot down over Yugoslavia during the UN peace operations to transport civilians evacuated from countries caught up in internal conflicts. These missions have demonstrated its potential for many types of missions.

OPERATION
Incorporated in Marine Expeditionary Units (MEU's) the CH-53E heavy helicopter's main objective is to supply heavy transport vehicles to the marine forces. In addition it transports teams of men and various kinds of material and equipment.

Development of the CH-53

The period of the SIKORSKY S-65, manufactured as the CH-53, was begun in October 1960 to satisfy a requirements of

ded to configure a vehicle with the capacity to transport a cargo of 3,630 kg over a distance of 111 miles at a speed of 167 mph. On the 24th of September 1962, after analyzing the proposals of Boeing, Kaman and Sikorsky, the Department of Defence made their decision known. They had decided to develop the SIKORSKY design, awarding the company 10 million dollars to construct a full-sized model, a fuselage for static trials and two prototypes for evaluation.

The first of the YCH-53A flew on the 14th of October 1964, and the evaluations continued without problems. The marines

the United States Marine Corps which was interested in a heavy helicopter vehicle to replace the Sikorsky HR2S-1/CH-37 Mojave, a model still propelled by radial engines.

Program

On the 7th of March 1962 the BuWeps (Bureau of Naval Weapons) published its requirements for program HH(X) (Helicopter, Heavy, eXperimental) which inten-

received the first batch of 141 CH-53A's in September 1965. Manufactured in the Connecticut factory, the production line continued with 20 CH-53C's for the United States Air Force, 126 CH-53D's for the marines and two CH-53's for the German Army which assembled twenty units in its own factories which were supplied in kit form, to which another 90 were added, manufactured under licence.

Adapted Versions

Other re-powered versions followed from the initial SEA STALLION units, modified for specific requirements, which included two VH-53D's assigned to carry the President of the United States, 47 HH-53H and MH-53J PAVE LOW units, used by the Air Force to carry out rescue missions for pilots shot down over enemy territory, for which they have received very complex equipment and weaponry. 34 MH-53E Sea Dragons were modified by the United States Marines to work as a towing vehicle using a system designed to neutralize naval mines, of these ten are in service with the Japanese Marines designated S-80M, with six more ending up in Iran. A hundred CH-53E Super Stallions, propelled by three jet engines are used in amphibious assault roles by 12 marine squadrons, bringing the total number produced up to 670 units, including two S-65Os, used during the seventies by the Austrian Air Force.

Added improvements

The Israeli firm MATA, of the Israel Aircraft Industries group, has been working since 1991 on the building of 40 units for the Israeli Airforce, initially A,C & D versions of the S-65, to a standard known as CH-53-2000. With a cost of 8 million dollars for each modified unit the modernized helicopters include a fixed nozzle for

DETAILS

A meteorological radar at its bow, fuel tanks mounted on the side of the fuselage, landing carriage consisting of three units with two wheels each, engines located in lateral gondolas, cockpit with good visibility, etc. These are the details which define the United States heavy helicopter.

COMPACT

Once the main rotor is folded up, the size of the SEA STALLION is noticeably reduced and is therefore easily fit into a hanger or amphibious vessel.

refueling in flight, two external tanks on fixed supports to hold 4,000 an additional liters of fuel, a self-defence system with interference flare-launchers, and electronic transmitters. Modifications to the cockpit instrumentation include multifunctional consoles and changes to allow the use of night vision goggles. There has also been a HOCAS system installed to control communication, a seat with controls for a flight engineer has also been included. With these alterations the maximum weight allowance has now increased to 22,680kg.

In combat

It has carried out infiltration missions with special troops during the Vietnam War, transported troops in operation Desert Storm, rescued Apollo crews from the sea, and captured equipment from Israeli commandos who had appropriated an entire SA-6 (Gainful) anti-aircraft missile battery. Evacuated residents in Liberia, Grenada and Albania. The Stallion family of helicopters has participated in two missions which are particularly noteworthy. The first, called Eagle Claw, took place on the 24th of April 1980 with the participation of eight RH-53D's of the United States Marines who tried to free a group of hostages held in Iran. The operation failed because two of them broke down in flight, and a third collided with a HERCULES assigned to do the refueling in flight. However, the second was carried out successfully by a CH-53E on the 2nd of June 1995, the operation was to recover Captain O'Grady who had been ejected over Banja Luka, in Serbian held territory, after his

F-16 was shot down during and aerial mission which was part of Operation Deny Flight.

Great capacity

The potential of the latest CH-53E ver-

THE DECK

The movement of CH-53E helicopters on the decks of amphibious vessels can be carried out with the support of special tow vehicles which facilitate their loading and positioning on the elevators.

move up to 16 tons hung from a sling which is hooked onto the underside of the fuselage.

Its design

The fuselage has a conventional semi-monohull made of aluminium, steel and tita-

CH-53E SUPER STALLION TECHNICAL CHARACTERISTICS

COST:	24.36 million dollars	**Maximum load**	16,330 kg
DIMENSIONS:		**Internal fuel**	3,849 l
Height	30.19 m	**External fuel**	4,921 l
Length	8.97 m	**PROPULSION:**	
Breadth	8.66 m	Three General Electric T64-GE-416 jet engines	
Turning surface area of main rotor	455.38 m²	with a joint maximum thrust of 13,140 horsepower	
Turning surface area of tail rotor	29.19 m²	**PERFORMANCE:**	
WEIGHT:		**Service ceiling height**	5,640 m
Empty	15,072 kg	**Maximum speed**	315 km/h
Maximum	33,450 kg	**Range**	2,075 km

sions is such that it is capable of carrying up to fifty soldiers with basic equipment, or it can

HOLD

Large and with a ramp in the stern which facilitates the entry of vehicles and cargo, the hold of the CH-53E is capable of accommodating fifty men or up to 14 tons of material, weapons or a variety of equipment.

nium, the cockpit has been manufactured with various combinations of glass fibres, other parts have been re-inforced with polyamide panels and titanium. It is a large craft and easily accessed thanks to the large rear door. This is operated hydraulically, which allows the easy entry and exit of men and material. This machine stands out for the internal space available, and its capacity to carry many types of cargo. And the placement of the main retractable landing gear in a lateral gondola equipped with shock-absorbers with a high absorption capacity.

The large tail at the back of the helicopter is slightly angled to the left, with an enormous stabilizer on its upper part. The tail section can be folded back to facilitate the positioning of the machine in transport vessels. In the lower part of the helicopter there are fenders which are automatically extended when the landing carriage is activated on landing. On the front right side there is an access door to the interior which in its upper part includes a winch to hoist small cargo or people during rescue missions.

Propulsion

Three General Electric T64-GE-416 or 419 jet engines are fitted to the machine. A large filter screen is incorporated into each engine casing. Together the engines are capable of producing a maximum thrust of 13,140 horsepower, with a transmission system capable of dealing with a take off loading of 13,500 horsepower. Two of these are located in lateral gondolas in the upper part of the fuselage and the third is incorporated in the structure above the engine, transmitting power to the main seven-bladed rotor and to the four-bladed tail rotor. The blade

---

TAIL

The tail which includes a four-bladed rotor and large stabilizer can be folded thanks to an automatic system incorporated in the helicopter.

PROPULSION

Between the cargo loading crane and the main rotor are the lateral gondolas fitted with enormous filters at the front to avoid the ingestion of all kinds of particles which two of the three jet engines draw in. The General Electric T64-GE-416 turbines constitute the propulsion plant of the CH-53E SUPER STALLION heavy helicopter.

---

folding system is automatically activated to reduce its size to the minimum.

To facilitate its maintenance various access and inspection panels have been incorporated into the structure it can also count on an electronic system which gives breakdown warnings and signals the need to replace various components. All of which improves the reliability of a machine which has demonstrated high operational readiness and a reduced number of accidents.

Equipment

Depending on the mission to be carried out, the different members of the CH-53 family can be equipped with a wide range of systems adapted for a particular mission. Usually the different transport variants turn to light and medium machine guns to give cover to personnel and material deployed. Those involved in crew rescue missions in hostile territory include; MINIGUN multibarrel machine guns capable of a rate of fire of 6000 rounds per minute, and other equipment such as radar and thermal imaging cameras with which they can fly at low altitudes to avoid being detected by enemy anti-aircraft systems; anti-mine units use a non-magnetic vehicle towed along the surface of the water. They are also equipped with a Westinghouse AN/AQS-14 sonar and usually fly equipped with interference flares and electronic disruption equipment for self-defence, using them when necessary. They can also be re-inforced with two types of guided missile: the STINGER or SIDEWINDER.

sales of the AS-330 PUMA helicopter, with 700 units produced and flying in many countries, it was decided to go ahead with the construction of an advanced version with a variety of improvements to the original model with the idea that it was to be more of a military than a civilian helicopter.

Evolution

The first preparatory studies by the French for a new version of this much appreciated transport helicopter began in 1974 and continued until a prototype was ready for trails, which first took place on the 13th of September 1978. After complying with a series of verification trials, the production phase for the AS-332 SUPER PUMA began halfway through 1981.

In July 1983 the L version with an elongated fuselage was certified and in 1986 the propulsion plant was modified with the introduction of the Turbomeca Makila IAI engines. The military versions produced from 1990 were given the designation AS-532 and called the Cougar to differentiate them from those machines destined for civilian operators.

Sales

The machines leaving the production line of the French company Aerospatiale, or those produced or assembled under licence in Indonesia, Spain, Turkey, or Switzerland are identified by a letter code which defines its characteristics and mode of use. As such U corresponds to unarmed units, A for armed, C for combat with a short fuselage, L for a long fuselage, and S for antisubmarine or anti-ship naval missions. Since 1992 the Mk2 has been sharing the production line with the older Mk1.

Nearly 500 units of different versions of this family have been ordered by close to seventy users in 67 countries, two thirds of which are for military use and 28 for VIP's (Very Important People). These include the UB/AB which has only been on offer for a short time, responding to the needs of the most modest of budgets.

The French defence industry knows how to optimize its aeronautical developments to satisfy the multiple requirements demanded by a variety of countries. Demonstrating with the Super Puma that it can design and manufacture transport helicopters with advanced capabilities to support ground, naval, or air operations. This has led to it having an impressive order book which it is predicted will grow with the new variations expected to be introduced in the next few years.

The conception of the helicopter

After the success encountered with

ADVANCED

The latest version created for military use is the AS 532 US which includes an elongated cabin with space for up to 29 soldiers; navigation systems, side winch, modified engine outlets etc which allow the most varied of missions to be carried out.

Military users

Among the most notable of the users are the French, who have specialized units such as the Horizon battlefield radar detector and the Mk2 U2 assigned to rescue work, the CSAR (Combat Search and Rescue), The Spanish who have ordered more than forty units for the Air Force and Ground Army, Abu Dhabi which uses five modified to have sonar and the capacity of launching EXOCET AM-39 anti-ship missiles and torpedoes, Turkey which operates twenty which it assembled under licence and there is a list of

ECONOMICAL
From the viewpoint of satisfying the needs of countries with low military budgets the COUGAR AS 532 UB/AB has been developed incorporating modifications to substantially reduce the purchase cost.

Conception

It has a large semi-monohull fuselage and is manufactured using a light aluminium alloy which acts as a base to be reinforced with titanium and composite materials. The front part is assigned for the flying of the craft, which requires one pilot in good visibility and two in times of IFR flight. In the center is the cargo hold and depending on the version, there is space for up to 25 soldiers and their personal equipment. In the back is the tail and rotor, on the sides the Messier-Bugatti landing carriage designed with high-

other countries which, amongst others, include Slovakia, Venezuela, Zaire, Oman, Brazil, Chile, The Netherlands, China, Ecuador, Panama, Mexico, Nepal, South Korea, Japan, and Germany which has assigned them to its border police.

The design

It is praised for its capacity to maintain operational with 98% effectiveness in support work ca-rried out on the North Sea oil platforms, yet criticized by others, such as pilots in Spain's Airborne Forces (FAMET) who don't consider it to be very satisfactory in its daily support role. The truth is that this French model is becoming more and more successful.

absorption parts to cope with possible ground impacts.

Five fuel tanks are positioned along the fuselage and under the cabin floor, with a capacity of 1,497 liters for the UC version and 2,141 for the SC version, it is possible, to install flexible cabin tanks to carry an additional 2000 liters additional, and with 2 exterior tanks, each holding 325 liters, it is capable of carrying out long range missions.

Propulsion

Located in the upper part of the fuselage and occupying a large part of its length, we find the propulsion unit with the two Turbomeca Makila IAI Jet Engines at the

to improve their resistance to impact and perforation. While the tail blades combine carbon fibres, resins and titanium.

There are two independent systems for operating the moving parts, and to connect them to the different flight control elements. Electrical energy is supplied by two 20kVA 400Hz alternators.

front. The design is a modular one with each turbine having a maximum power of 1,877 horsepower, integrating air intakes with filters in front to prevent the ingestion of ice and foreign objects. Some models have been modified to reduce the infra-red signature. Mk2 models are supplied with the Makila IA2, with 2,109 horsepower.

The engines turn the transmission system up to 23,840 revolutions per minute and transmit their power to the main rotor which turns at 265 r.p.m. and to the tail rotor at 1,278 r.p.m. The four main blades are completely articulated and have been manufactured with elastomers

Great capability

It was originally designed to transport troops with combat equipment, which it can do using individual seats or with sol-

diers seated on the fuselage floor. Different versions are offered which support its capacity to receive different weapon systems or to move weights up to 4.5 tons hung from a sling. Machine guns can be set up on the mounts inside the aircraft for its self-defence, and on the outside walls it is possible to mount 20mm GIAT monotube cannons, 68mm rocket-launchers, light torpedoes, Exocet or Sea Skua anti-ship missiles etc.

Amongst some of the more noteworthy models are the VIP version, with an optimized cabin to transport important people in the greatest comfort possible, battlefield surveillance units with the Horizon antenna system located in the lower back part of the fuselage, and naval support units with a variety of sonar equipment including sonar buoy launchers, and display consoles. The rescue CSAR, used in France and Saudi Arabia incorporates a fixed nozzle for in-flight refueling, and a side winch for hoisting loads up to 272 kg, optics for night time flights and search missions, auxiliary floats built into the lateral landing carriages, weapon mounts, and a cockpit with digital displays and the most modern equipment, making it possible to rescue two pilots in a zone located 500 miles from the departure point and to be able to return to base without refueling in flight, something

SELF-PROTECTION

Peace missions, as executed by this machine assigned to the United Nations, require the use of flare-launchers to interfere with the seeker head of anti-aircraft missiles (photograph above).

SPECIALIZATION

Two COUGAR AS 532 UL units are assigned to transport the Horizon battlefield detection system which can simultaneously process the information coming from 4,000 targets (photograph to the right).

which, if done, would considerably increase this distance.

TRANSPORT

Assuming the most varied of missions the French COUGAR helicopters have been specifically designed to transport troops and support elements in every kind of military operation (photograph on the left).

AS 532SC TECHNICAL CHARACTERISTICS

COST:	14 million dollars		Maximum external load	4,500 kg
DIMENSIONS:			Internal fuel	2,141 l
Fuselage length	15.53 m		PROPULSION:	
Height	4.92 m		Two Turbomeca Makila 1A1 jet engines with	
Main rotor diameter	15.60 m		a combined power of 3,754 horsepower	
Main rotor turning area	191.13 m²		PERFORMANCE:	
Cockpit surface area	7.8 m²		Service ceiling height	4,100 m
WEIGHT:			Stationary ceiling height	2,800 m
Empty	4,500 kg		Maximum speed	278 km/h
Maximum	9,350 kg		Range	870 km

COCKPIT

The most advanced features of the COUGAR cockpit include four large digital presentation screens and numerous indicators associated with the various flight parameters , elements which facilitate the work of the pilots located in this front part of the fuselage.

WEAPONRY

Simple mounts on the inside of the cockpit allow the personnel transporter to employ light and medium machine guns with greater accuracy, although when it is necessary lateral mounts can be adapted for more significant weapons.

CABLE CUTTERS

An extremely sharp blade is incorporated in the front part of the fuselage to cut all kinds of cables, avoiding accidents as a result of low altitude flight.

LANDING CARRIAGE

The front of the retractable londing carriage inclu- des two small wheels, located below the cockpit, while the two main elements are located on the sides and are drawn up into the lateral modules on the fuselage.

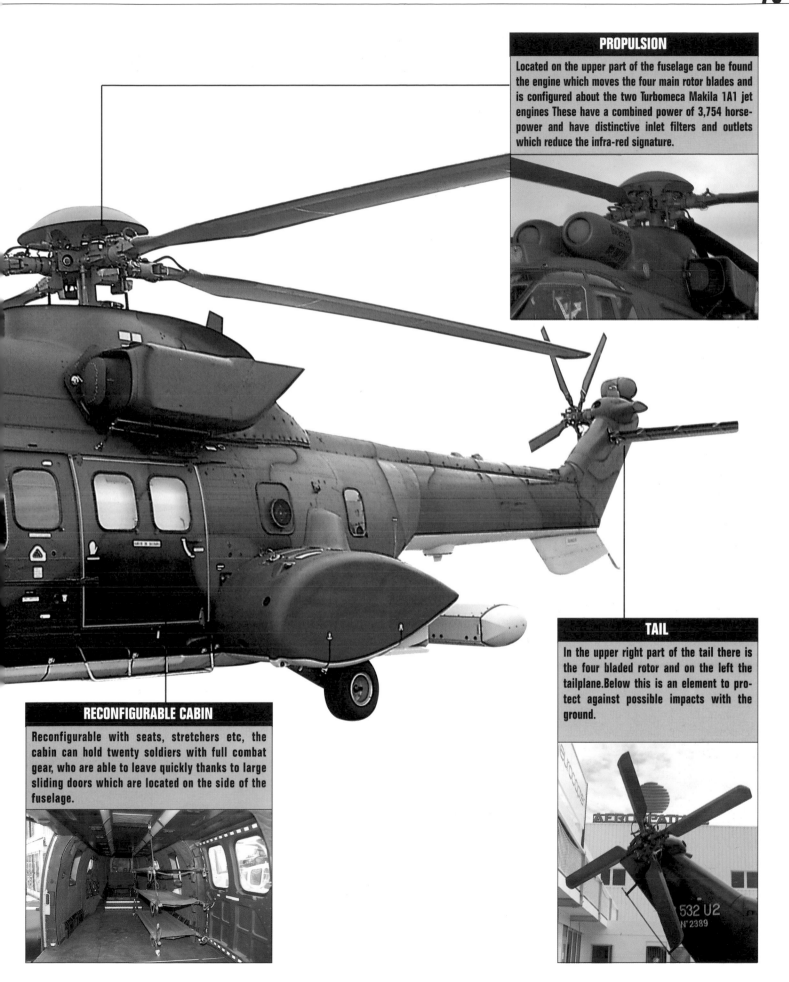

PROPULSION

Located on the upper part of the fuselage can be found the engine which moves the four main rotor blades and is configured about the two Turbomeca Makila 1A1 jet engines These have a combined power of 3,754 horsepower and have distinctive inlet filters and outlets which reduce the infra-red signature.

TAIL

In the upper right part of the tail there is the four bladed rotor and on the left the tailplane.Below this is an element to protect against possible impacts with the ground.

RECONFIGURABLE CABIN

Reconfigurable with seats, stretchers etc, the cabin can hold twenty soldiers with full combat gear, who are able to leave quickly thanks to large sliding doors which are located on the side of the fuselage.

of nearly every country in the world. Making these aircraft indispensable in modern walfare.

Introduction

The German and United States developments made during the second world war brought about the introduction of the helicopter to virtually every kind of military operation.

Capability

Although the first evaluations and missions took place in the last part of the second world war, it was during the Korean War that the process of introducing helicopters to carry out the most varied of tasks began. At first, the Vought-Sikorsky-5 and the Bell M47 were deployed for medical evacuation and reconnaissance missions, although with the arrival of the Sikorsky S-55, transport and rescue missions began. Because of the size of its hold it was able to move squads of soldiers to different parts of the front.

The experiences of the United States, together with those of the French in Indochina, led it to studying, under the leadership of Colonel Jay Vanderpool, the different mission possibilities for this kind of machine. The idea was for it to be used as some kind of air cavalry. These types of missions were complemented by the French in Algeria where they used the Piasecki H-21, by the British who deployed soldiers using the Bristol Sycamore to fight against guerrillas in Cyprus, and by the United States in Vietnam.

Developments in the evolution of different helicopters have resulted in the introduction of multiple tasks in all kinds of airborne missions, with the objective of transporting men, material, and weapon systems.

To carry out these missions specific models have been configured and other multi-purpose units adapted, thus making the helicopter a versatile aircraft that is widely used at the moment by the armies

MULIPLIER

The capacity of the Chinook CH-47 to transport artillery pieces, ammunition and equipment means that with three helicopters a battery placement can be changed quickly and efficiently in only a few minutes.

MULTIPURPOSE

Troop infiltration , transport of units, logistical re-supplies, medical evacuations and others are executed without problems by various helicopters.

CAPACITY

Transport helicopter enjoy a large cargo capacity, a great deal can be stored in the hold-hung in slings that are especially efficient during the execution of airborne operations.

Air Cavalry

The strange scenario of Vietnam, with forces from the North and South in conflict, led the United Sates which was participating in the war, to begin deploying every kind of helicopter in support of the

BOSNIA

British Commando helicopters, manufactured by Westland, are working to facilitate the transportation of troops and material assigned to the IFOR forces in the former Yugoslavia.

most varied of missions. The machines from the UH-1 family were converted to multi-purpose use which could infiltrate up to surveillance lines where, with machine gun fire and rockets, they were able to attack the enemy in their placements or whilst on maneuvers.

It was in this conflict that the concepts and use of the Air Cavalry were definitely established and understood, with the helicopter becoming indispensable when it was necessary to rescue pilots who had been shot down. Models such as the Sikorsky CH-3 and the CH-53 Sea Stallion and the CH-46 SEA KNIGHT were employed for the transportation of artillery pieces, medical evacuations, logistical support and moving contingents. Demonstrating their multi-purpose capacity, even though many were lost to enemy light arm and anti-aircraft fire.

Assault operations

A lot of experience has been gained and been consequently drawn upon and applied to new specialized design models to incorporate solutions to face lessen its vulnerability. Such as the protection of certain areas of the craft or the installation of tanks with reduced risk during strong ground impacts.

Although the Airborne Forces of the Spanish Army actively employed its transport machines during combat against Moroccan and Polisario factions in the early years of the 1970's. The most important helicopter transport mission after Vietnam took place in the Caribbean island of Grenada in October 1983, where helicopters transported a large part of the United States Rangers and Marines that participated in the initial assault. Although some machines were lost, the experience served to consolidate the concept and in various countries battalions or brigades have appeared which specialize in air

PARACHUTISTS

The Soviet Mi-17-1V heavy helicopter was employed to allow parachutist infiltration to attack sensitive points and facilitate the operations of air assault groups (photograph above).

HELICOPTER TRANSPORTERS

The massive use of various kinds of transport machines with different capabilities requires great co-ordination to guarantee the best assault operation possible and the lowest number of injuries.

transport assault missions, deployed using planes or helicopters.

The idea of using helicopters reached its climax during the Gulf war in 1991 against Iraq, in which missions of special importance were entrusted to the United States XVIII Air Transport Army Corps which included 2 brigades, the 82nd Air Transport Division and 101st Air Assault Division. These units were actively employed against the towns of Salman and Samawa, located on the left flank of the main front.

The doctrine of employment

The use of helicopters has been consolidated over the last thirty years, but the doctrine of employing them in airborne missions has been changing with the appearance of new models and the establishment of new needs and operational requirements.

A variety of missions

Classified as light, medium or heavy as a result of their cargo capacity, helicopters

can be employed in tactical roles in logistics thanks to their high level of mobility and flexibility. Tactical transporters are involved in moving troops to points where maximum concentrations of men are required to carry out determined pushes to occupy important positions or key routes, to carry out surprise attacks, anti-guerilla operations, the interception of enemy troops, covering flanks and the logistics designed to transport material,

which is either dropped off at the required point or launched over the mission zone.

Infiltration capacity

Although the rotation of helicopter rotors is easily identifiable by radar operators, valleys, mountain formations, trees, etc. allow them to take advantage of irregularities in the terrain by low level flights which minimize the risk of being located by specialised systems.

NEEDS

Helicopters have proven themselves to be indispensable in supporting different ground force missions, in areas such as supply work, facilitating maneuvers and the needs of the moment.

INFILTRATION

Commandos on special missions can be infiltrated quickly and later taken out by other helicopters.

Air transport basics

War operations require rapid movements of troops and material to take advantage of offensive action and to also improve defensive missions. These fundamentally involve medium and heavy transport helicopters to carry troops to where their services are required.

Many of the operations are executed at night to avoid being visually located, and normally the noise of the engines is not appreciable until the last moment.

Helicopters are ideal for reconnaissance missions over long distances, the infiltration of combat patrols, the capturing of equipment and enemy personnel etc. and missions that require the transportation of small groups of specialists to the mission zone for deployment, and finally to pick up men after carrying out their mission.

These types of machine are basically multipliers of logistical capacity, transporting ammunition, supplies, fuel etc. to different units, or they constitute mobile centers of support which advance with ground forces. Also important are theirheavy transportation capacities with existing models like the United States Super Stallion and Russian Mil Mi-26 which are capable of moving anything from artillery pieces up to light armored track vehicles, hung from slings or stored inside the helicopter. This is to act in a support capacity or to vary the position of artillery batteries by towing them away from enemy fire.

Designers were led to incorporate a space in ship constructions to accommodate the transport, maintenance and operation of specialized helicopters. This came from the need to provide surface naval units such as frigates or destroyers with additional capacity in the search, location, and disabling of enemy ships. These can also be deployed from amphibious vessels, and aircraft carriers.

Assigned to special missions, naval helicopters carry out an important role, increasing the possibilities of action for the units they are deployed from. Giving greater capacity to carry out anti-submarine (ASW) and surface-to-surface actions together tasks which are complemented by other secondary activities such as long distance reconnaissance, re-supplying, medical evacuations "MEDEVAC" (MEDical EVACuation), the transport of personnel etc.

The Introduction of the helicopter

After the second world war, the process of introducing helicopters began with the

> **MULTINATIONAL**
> The NH90 helicopter is the fruit of a multinational project to produce a family of advanced naval helicopters which could satisfy the specific needs of the marines of France, Italy, Germany and The Netherlands.

> **ADAPTED**
> The "Lynx" helicopter has been adapted to carry out naval activities for which it has received very advanced specialized equipment which has favored it in exports markets.

idea of them being appropriate for various phases of combat, including naval missions. The need for these machines to supply the marines of various European nations led to their co-manufactuer in the 1950's, under a United States design licence. This was an advantageous experience with the modernizing of models and the creation of new machines adapted from the needs highlighted in the development stages.

Evolution

The British company Westland obtained a licence in 1959 for the manufactuer of the United States Sikorsky S-61/SH-3 SEA KING. The company began to manufactuer and supply them to the Royal Navy as a heavy helicopter capable of executing anti-submarine tasks. Developing it through the years into specialized versions for use in anti-submarine warfare (ASW) and in an airbourne early warning role using the Thorn-EMI Searchwater radar and as transporter for the Royal Marine comandos. Its manufactuer has exceeded 325 units, it is also employed by the marines of Germany, India, Pakistan, Australia, and Egypt.

Later, the Italian company Agusta Spa obtained the license to manufacture the 212 model as an anti-submarine variant. This was as a result of its experience in constructing, under license, the Sikorsky SH-3 and various models of the United States Bell Company. Known as the AB-212, this twin-turbine model incorporates modified avionics and different equipment to allow it to act as a submarine hunter or anti-ship helicopter, of which more than a hundred units have been manufactured for the marines of Italy, Greece, Turkey, Spain, and Venezuela. Spain has incorporated a dozen of these including four which have been modified to carry out electronic support missions using the Colibri system.

JOINT MANUFACTURED

The LYNX was born as the result of the relationship between British and French companies, and is usually deployed on French frigates and destroyers, equipped with a landing pad and maintenance hanger.

WIDESPREAD

The Agusta Bell 212's have been exported to numerous countries including Spain which has incorporated a dozen of them in its Third Air Force Navy Squadron for transport, electronic warfare, and naval surface and search missions.

Own capability

Previous developments, along with other important aspects, brought about the birth of their own designs which benefited from previous manufacturing experience. Together with the process of optimization and adaptation of the models in service. The first to be conceived was the Lynx which was born as the fruit of a collaboration between France and Great Britain- 30% the former and 70% the latter. Entering production in 1976 after nine years in development, the Lynx has since been adopted in its specialized naval form by Germany, Great Britain, France, Portugal, Brazil, Argentina, Egypt, The Netherlands, Denmark, South Korea, and Nigeria, with more than a hundred machines in service. The Lynx and the Super Lynx specialize in A.S.W. air-to-surface actions. The latter of the two being an updated model equipted with the most modern and advanced technology.

In 1979 an agreement was signed between Westland and Agusta for the development of a new helicopter to replace the Sea King and the lynx. After creating a joint company known as European Helicopter Industries. They began the work of constructing the EH-101 Merlin which flew for the first time in October 1987. The first units entered service in 1998 in British and

Italian ships. There are as of yet sales to other countries such as Canada or Spain, which could substitute these for existing helicopters.

Other specific versions have been produced for naval use like the SUPER FRELON, the Eurocopter AS 365N3 Dauphin 2, or the NHI Industries NH90 destined to equip future frigates for France, Italy, Germany and The Netherlands.

THE DUTCH

The Dutch Marines, as in other countries, are operating with the naval version of the LYNX, which has demonstrated itself ideal for the purpose despite its small size and reduced tactical possibilities.

SPECIALIZATION

The Italian Marines actively employ their AB-212's in anti-submarine work from surface ships. Work which will be done by the MERLIN in the future.

Their details

Each one conceived at a different time and with the objective of meeting different operating requirements, their characteristics differ in size, mission possibilities, equipment and tactical use.

The "Sea King"

Manufactured in Italy and Great Britain, it has the capacity to hunt and destroy its target which allows it to operate independently from surface ships. It was conceived around a large core which included a cockpit at the front for the pilot and co-pilot, a lower part which allows it to make emergency landings on water, two lateral elements which are home to the main landing carriage, which is retracted during flight, and a large free area where up to 22 people can travel and also where different kinds of equipment can be put.

The British machines are equiped with a GEC-Marconi AQS-902G-DS processor associated with the 2069 sonar, a sonar buoy launcher, AN/ASQ-50 magnetic anomalies detector, a display screen for the systems operator, surface search operations are carried out by an integrated navigation system whose main component is the Thomson Thron AR15955 Radar.

Powered by two Rolls Royce Gnome H-1.400-IT Jet Engines which together give

TECHNICAL CHARACTERISTICS

	AB-212 ASW	"Sea King"	"Lynx"	"Merlin"
COST IN MILLIONS OF DOLLARS:	12	14	22	35
DIMENSIONS:				
Fuselage length	17.4 m	22.15 m	15.165 m	22.81 m
Height	4.53 m	5.13 m	3.48 m	6.62 m
Main rotor diameter	14.63 m	18.90 m	12.80 m	18.59 m
Main rotor turning area	173.9 m²	280.48 m²	128.71 m²	271.51 m²
WEIGHTS:				
Empty	3,240 kg	5,447 kg	2,740 kg	7,121 kg
Maximum	5,070 kg	9,752 kg	4,876 kg	14,600 kg
Maximum arms load	800 kg	1,300 kg	700 kg	960 kg
Fuel	814 l	3,714 l	957 l	3,222 l
PROPULSION PLANT POWER	1,875 CV	3,320 CV	2,240 CV	6.936 CV
PERFORMANCE:				
Ceiling service height	4,023 m	1.705 m	3,230 m	5,000 m
Maximum speed	196 km/h	272 km/h	232 km/h	278 km/h
Range	667 km	1,482 km	500 km	900 km

the 3,320 horsepower necessary to give agility to the main five-bladed rotor, it can be fitted with a BL10300 side winch with the capacity to hoist loads of up to 272 kg, or with a varied range of launchable weaponry. In the case of the British units this include up to four STING RAY search torpedoes, four MKII depth charges, two Sea Eagle anti-ship missiles, and a medium support machine gun installed in a lateral mount, which is operated from inside the helicopter.

The AB-212 ASW

Manufactured in Italy by Agusta, this derivative of AB-205 for naval use incorporates various changes to the core which allow it to be adapted to different operating requirements. Important for working over the surface of the sea is the Pratt & Whitney Canada PT6T-6 Turbo Twin Pac, a tin twin jet engine which produces 1,875 horsepower with reduced consumption, which allows the machine to stay in the air for up to 3 hours.

The specialized equipment of these Italian units consists of a MM/APS-705 surface search radar located in a cylindrical housing above the cockpit, an AQS-18 sonar unit of variable depth and low fre-

> **ESPECIALIZATION**
> The latest versions of the British Super Lynx are equipped with the most advanced electronic systems including a thermal imaging camera, surface search radar and a complex front assembly which differentiates it from other members of this family.

> **JOINT MANUFACTURED**
> The LYNX was born as the result of the relationship between British and French companies, and is usually deployed on French frigates and destroyers, equipped with a landing pad and maintenance hanger.

quency and an operator screen. With a reinforced core for improved resistance to marine corrosion, skids supplied with floats for emergency landings on the sea surface, and strengthening for berthing under cover. It has surpassed other more modern designs and has been consigned to various fleets, such as Spain's. It carries out other secondary missions such as transportation, liaison work, surface searches, and tasks involving the use of rocket launchers, Whitehead A-244/S anti-submarine torpedoes, mines or anti-ship missiles such as the Marte MK2.

The "Lynx"

Compact and with great agility in the air, this small British-French helicopter is based on a one-piece fuselage constructed of light alloy, with doors, tailplane and access panels made from glass fibre. Its characteristics are: a three-wheeled non-retractable undercarriage, a cockpit equipped with the most advanced equipment which gives it a high capability, a compact propulsion plant consisting of two Rolls Royce Gem2 Jet Engines with a combined power of 2,240 horsepower, and in the case of one of them failing, a system to increase the power in one to the maximum possible. Capable of carrying 10 men or for storing equipment particular to the navy.

The British helicopters have (GPS) global positioning systems; GEC-Marconi A15979 Seaspray MK1 Search Radar with the capability to locate small targets in conditions of low visibility and rough sea conditions, Bendix sonar equipment; Sea Owl thermal imaging cameras; radar emission detectors etc. The French units are armed with Mk46 and Murene light torpedoes, depth charges and AS-15TT anti-ship missiles.

The "Merlin"

Belonging to the third generation, the EH101 is a large helicopter for those fleets which require a wide range of possibilities for search activities associated with their defence. Created mainly with an aluminium and lithium fuselage, composite materials, and sandwich type panels. Its missions are mainly to search for and neutralize surface naval units and submarines, for which the

COMPLEX

The complexity of the equipment installed in the anti-submarine helicopters means that highly qualified personnel are required to do the maintenance and installation work done in the stern hangers of frigates and destroyers.

HEAVY DUTY

The French "Super Frelon" has carried out multiple naval missions, and amongst which is the noteworthy anti-ship hunter version equipped with powerful "EXOCET" missiles located in lateral mounts.

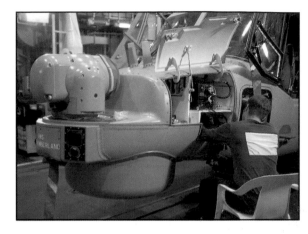

fuselage has been developed so that it is big enough to be fitted out with the specialized equipment and weaponry necessary. At the same time it is small enough to be able to fit into the small hangers of frigates.

It is capable of operating from its carrier ship in winds of up to 54 mph and in sea conditions of gale force 6. Incorporating an automatic hook up system to the flight deck. Its main rotor can adopt a negative angle of incidence to facilitate landing in extreme conditions, in which the five-bladed main rotor is very useful, driven by Rolls Royce/Turbomeca RTM322 Jet Engines, producing a combined power of 6,936 horsepower.

Installed in Martin Baker Armored Seats, two crew members work in a cockpit which includes six display screens in Litton Color, while the operator of the acoustic surveillance system and observer travel in the cabin behind, which is also equipped with a display console with four monitors. Thanks to this it is simple to control the GEC-Marconi Blue Kestrel Search Radar, the AQS-903 acoustic processor associated with the Thomson-Sintra Sonar System which extends to a depth of 600 metres. The Racal Electronic Components Support System which identify and locate hostile radar, the JTIDS coded link; the attack equipment which, with a maximum load of 960 kg, includes four light search torpedoes, two anti-ship missiles, depth charges, and machine guns for self-defence decoy to confuse the heads of guided missiles.

United States naval strategists wanted to achieve dominance of the seas, especially when taking into account the important growth of the Soviet Submarine Fleet. This led them, in the 1950's, to begin a strengthening program which principally

The introduction of different models

With the objective of carrying out the needs of specialized machines, various models entered service from the beginning of the 1950's, some of the better known ones being the Piasechi HUP-2S Retriever, the HRS-2 and HSS-1 Seabat. After experimenting with these designs the United States Navy, in December 1957, contracted the firm Sikorsky for the manufactuer of ten units of an advanced design, designated YHSS-2, the first of which flew on the 11th of March 1959, resulting in the SH-3A Sea King-equally capable of hunting and destroying in flight.

resulted in the establishment of a powerful group of aircraft carriers to carry squadrons to wherever they were needed.

To protect them and to provide coverage for transport ships, it was planned to put into service escort ships such as frigates and destroyers, supplied with helicopters which were specialized in the work of detecting and destroying enemy submarines.

Acquisition

SEA KINGS were equipped with a Bendix AQS Sonar System and Ryan APN-130 Doppler Radar managed by two operators located in the cabin. In parallel to the first 254 units contracted and entering service, there were also the first Kaman HU-2A Seasprite light helicopters, which were assigned to the role of navy search and rescue.

After removing the ASW aircraft carriers from the ranks of the US Navy it was decided to optimize the SEA KING. In 1967 the modernized SH-3D version entered service with more powerful engines and more modern systems, such as the AQS sonar and APN-182 Doppler Radar. The introduction of the LAMPS (Light Airborne Multi Purpose System) came about by the contracting of twenty modified Seasprite helicopters at the beginning of the seventies in the anti-submarine SH-2D standard. Incorporating a Canadian Marconi LN-66HP Surface Radar located below the cockpit, a Texas Instruments ASQ-81 Magnetic Anomaly Detector (MAD), a 15 tube launcher of sonar buoys, active and passive. A mounting for the carrying of two light torpedoes, all of which are controlled by a system specialist.

Improvements introduced

Later and up to 1982, another hundred of the standard SH-2F units were modified.

"SEASPRITE"
Two United States Navy Fleet Reserve squadrons continue using the SH-2F in submarine detection missions and general naval support, missions which will continue up to the middle of the next decade.

ANTI-BOAT
The use of the "Penguin" AGM-119B from SEAHAWK light helicopters gives it the capability to reach naval units located some 18 miles away, adding additional capacity to transport other arms for subsequent attacks.

At the same time that helicopters were being incorporated with a new rotor and modifications to the retractable undercarriage, 116 SH-3H's were being introduced, modified with new radar, sonar and dipole scatterers to confuse older systems. Later it was decided to eliminate some equipment to be able to install new tactical navigation systems and to give it the sonar buoy processor capability.

As a result of the 1982 budget the manufactuer of eighteen SH-60B Seahawk LAMPS MkIII units was begun, a concept which had been validated since 1979 with five prototypes. The entry into service of this advanced platform allowed some SH-3H's to be retired, with the former being introduced to aircraft carriers from 1991.

The close protection Battle Group SH-60F model, with an SH-60R version from 1998, was developed with improved protection to equip modern destroyers. Also ready from 1998 is the Super Seasprite SH-2G optimized with the most advanced cockpit which includes Litton modern display screens, front facing infra-red trackers, equipped with the capability to use anti-boat missiles such as the Kongsberg Penguin AGM-119 B.

The users

Many countries have followed the example of the United States Navy, which has been equipped with early models in their modernized versions, with improved capabilities.

TECHNICAL CHARACTERISTICS

	SH-3D "SEA KING"	SH-2F "SEASPRITE"	SH-60B "SEAHAWK"
COST IN MILLIONS OF DOLLARS:	14	12	20,25
DIMENSIONS:			
Length	22.21 m	16.03 m	19.76 m
Height	5.13 m	4.72 m	5.18 m
Main rotor diameter	18.90 m	13.41 m	16.36 m
Main rotor turning area	280.48 m²	141.26 m²	210.14 m²
WEIGHT:			
Empty	5,447 kg	3,193 kg	6,191 kg
Maximum	9,752 kg	6,123 kg	9,926 kg
Maximum arms loading	1,300 kg	500 kg	500 kg
Fuel	3,714 l	1,779 l	2,233 l
Propulsion plant power	3,320 CV	2,700 CV	3,380 CV
PERFORMANCE:			
Ceiling service height	4,410 m	6,860 m	5,790 m
Maximum speed	272 km/h	230 km/h	272 km/h
Range	1,482 km	661 km	600 km

The SEASPRITE continues flying in the United States and Argentine Naval Air Reserve. The "Super Seasprite" has been purchased by Egypt, New Zealand and Australia. Australia, like Spain, Japan, Greece, Thailand, and Taiwan operates different versions of the SH-60, with two hundred in the navy. With respect to the SH-3, these are in service in Argentina, Australia, Brazil, Germany, Belgium, India, Japan, Pakistan, Peru, and Spain, among others.

Different capabilities

Designed in accordance with different requirements, in distinct periods and incorporating very different electronics and detection systems, the capabilities of the various models analysed differ greatly.

Advanced models

Without doubt the most advanced and

CAPABILITY

Multipurpose and powerful, the SH-3 heavy helicopter is carrying out service on different naval missions. It is a very effective machine in the search for submarines, a task which it carries out in some of the countries which are using it.

expensive of them all is the SEAHAWK which employs a well proven and successful concept, including two powerful navy General Electric jet engines, type T700-GE-410, a RAST recovery system which facilitates landings on escort ship platforms and employ very advanced avionics. Their different configurations include surface search radar, sonar equipment including sonar buoy launchers, magnetic anomaly detectors, acoustic processors, etc. All of which can easily detect any threat, transmitting the information to the carrier ship via a coded communication link, and allowing it to disable the target with its own weapons, or with those of the associated ships.

Continuing with this theme the SUPER SEASPRITE has recently been modernized at remarkably low cost. It now offers a very satisfactory capability with its new equipment and is able to carry out multiple naval hunt missions. The different SEA KING models take a back-seat role despite being modernized. A fact which results from their design and size. Although some units are being directed to complementary activities such as carrying aerial detection systems or the transport of commandos on infiltration missions.

High Powered

The capability of the on board equip-

ment is such that it allows the detection of submerged targets or others on the sea surface. But it can do more than detect these targets because the helicopter also has the capability of attacking them its own weapons, these being fixed on laeral mounts on the fuselage and which are specifically designed to carry a whole array of weapon systems. Submerged targets can be neutralized by using Mk-46-5 and Mk-50 light torpedoes which also include a guidance system capable of taking them up to the objective. The aircraft also carriers depth charges which are designed to explode on contact or alternatively at a pre-determined depth. PENGUIN and AGM-114 HELLFIRE Anti-ship Missiles can be used to attack surface targets, these being guided towards the target by using the helicopter's radar tracking system. The 70 mm rockets carried are also very effective particularly when they are fired in salvos against unprotected ship structures. The use of machine gun fire is also an extremely useful weapon, being able to damage very important auxiliary equipment such as radar electronic systems. All of these variations give this helicopter a

CAPABILITY

A radar detector below the cockpit and lateral launcher for up to 15 sonar buoys, and light torpedo mount, etc are some of the characteristics which define the SH-2 in its role as a submarine hunter.

"SEAHAWK"

Considered to be the most sophisticated and advanced anti-submarine helicopter in the world, the SH-60 can carry out other missions such as searching the sea surface and neutralizing naval units. As such it is a truly multipurpose naval machine.

weapons system which is able to offer a wealth of different options depending on the country using them, the conditions, and the mission assigned at that time.

It was for features such as these that the SH-60 was used extensively during the Gulf War. Its function was to act as a surface exploration platform being specially equipped with a coded video link which allowed it to transmit real time information captured by its infra-red cameras to its own naval units. An attack was then launched against the target missions in which light machine guns were used as a self-defence measure when faced with possible interceptions by small patrol boats and ships.

Machine guns and cannons

Although it is possible to fire infantry weapons through the access doors of the majority of helicopters, images which were widespread during the time of the Vietnam War when troops fired their Colt M-16 guns at the ground looking for possible Vietcong soldiers. A series of mounts have been designed which allow a more rational use of every kind of machine gun from light 5.56mm, medium 7.62mm, to heavy 12.7mm. The most simple has a lateral fixing, and a ball and socket joint which facilitates the transversal movement of the weapon. This is a low cost, easy to install system. There are more complex assemblies in existence such as those of the Belgian company FN used with MAG 58 Machine Guns, the United States M134 with six rotating barrels which fires 7.62x51mm ammunition at a rate of fire of up to 6000 rounds per minute, or the machine gun mounts designed by Fabrica de Artilleria (FABA) of the Spanish company Bazán providing a self-defence capacity for SH-60 naval helicopters, which the Spanish Navy deployed to Persian Gulf waters during DESERT STORM. Highlighting with these that they can attack unprotected targets in a radius of less than a kilometer. In all of these a simple aiming system for the target was used, in which there was more hope in the salvos fired than in the accuracy actually obtained.

More powerful than those previously mentioned are the 20 or 30mm cannons which are used from mounts fixed on the fuselage, as well as from turrets incorporated in the transporter. Among those mentioned earlier is the 20mm Rheinmetall Rh-202,

The need to carry out support missions for ground force units brings with it, from the first moment, the need to install a variety of already existing weapons on those helicopter models being put into service. For example, the 7.92mm Rheinmetall MG15 Machine Gun which was mounted in the German Focker-Achgelis FA223 DRACHE Helicopters in 1944.

Today, after evaluating in combat many different concepts, the specialized systems introduced have been widely spread, with

> **MACHINE GUNS**
> A simple and light mount allows the use of medium machine guns like this 7.62mm FN from the side windows of the "Black Hawk" transport helicopter.

> **EFFECTIVENESS**
> The power, rate of fire and accuracy of machine guns convert them into simple pieces of equipment to use against ground positions. They are economical to use because of the kind of ammunition used.

launch systems covering a range of weaponry, from air-to-surface or air-to-air, depending on whether the mission involves ground targets or the hunting of surface naval units or submarines.

> **CAPABILITY**
> The ability of a 30mm projectile to penetrate laminated armored plating, is clearly shown from this shot, and gives us an idea of the effectiveness against light and lightly armored vehicles.

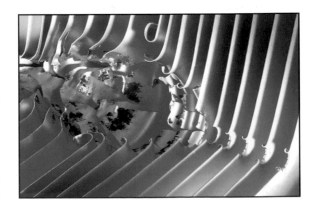

employed by the Spanish Bo-105's from a mount located in the lower part of the fuselage, and fed from a drum located in the cargo hold. The 20mm Oerlikon KAA evaluated in the British LYNXs, the Russian 23mm, the GIAT M621 used in the French PUMA family of machines. The second group belongs to the United States M197 tri-barrelled assembly used in the COBRA, the United States 30mm M230 CHAIN GUN used in the APACHE. The 30mm Russian 2A42 installed in the Russian Mi-28 HAVOC, which has an effective range of just over a mile.

Rocket Launchers and other systems

With their simplicity of use, various models of rocket-launchers can be located in lateral mounts on the sides of the transporter and aiming can be done by orientating the launcher with respect to the objective. To improve accuracy it is normal to turn to the use of time fused heads, or to those which include multiple munitions which hit wider areas of terrain. Noting that once the rockets are launched the helicopter may take evasive action, maneuvering in such a way as to avoid the response of adversaries.

Although, models are manufactured which go from 37 up to 81mm, the most normal is to turn to 68 and 70mm- or 2.75", of which the market offers many options, fired from launchers which usually have from 2 to 19 cells. From these, and thanks to electrical activation, various rocket models can be fired, among which are the Canadian CRV7 with an explosive head of 4.5 kilo-

TRANSFORMATION

A couple of sub-wing supports and various machine gun and rocket housings can be fixed converting the Sikorsky S-76 light helicopter into a powerful machine capable of providing support fire (photograph above).

SIMPLICITY

The machine gun is the most simple of weapons and it can be employed effected from lateral mounts or from assemblies operated inside the helicopter.

HOUSING

Built onto the side of the fuselage the medium machine gun housings constitute an additional fire power to support the missions of its own ground forces.

grams, Brazilian SBAT-70, Greek Mk4 model 10, French Matra SNEB, Russian series S-8, United States Hydra 70 and Mk40, Argentinian CBAS and the different versions of the Swedish SNORA. It is also possible to find different rocket housing models which combine machine guns and rockets in the mount.

Additionally, in many models containers can be hung from the slings which allow the programmed launch of anti-tank mines, such as DAT from the Italian company Tecnovar, or arms can de deployed depending on the circumstances. Airships have on some occasions dropped mortar grenades above

enemy positions. Also well known is the use of 40mm automatic grenade launchers in lateral mounts, amongst which is the noteworthy United States M-94, which fires grenades at a rate of 400 per minute although, any model offered on the market can be fitted on the lateral fixings.

Missiles

Fundamental to the missions of modern attack machines, the missile equipment

consists of air-to-ground anti-tank launchers and anti-aircraft launchers. The missiles are normally located in housings which are loaded onto the side mounts and which require the installation of a specific guidance system which can be anything from the simple head of an optical visor, for a variety of weapons, to a complex system which incorporates a laser rangefinder with optical vision systems.

MULTIPURPOSE

The gyro-stabilized viewfinder located in the bow of this Hughes 500 allows it to work with the two TOW guided missiles which are transported on its left side in the same way that the machine gun is installed in the housing on the right side.

Missiles are classified as long range if they are capable of covering 2.5 miles or very long range if they can cover a greater distance. Among the different models there is the Multinational HOT 1&2, produced by the German-French company Aerospatiale; the United States BGM-71 TOW widely proven on a variety of platforms and the AGM-114 HELLFIRE which is guided to the target by its laser head or by a system which follows

GRENADE LAUNCHERS

Automatic and belt fed, this United States M-94 assembly is operated by one gunner and is capable of firing at a rate of up to 400 grenades of 40x53mm per minute.

particular thermal signatures. The Chinese Honjian 8, the South African SWIFT, the Russian AT-6 SPIRAL, of which the Mi-28 is capable of carrying up to 16. There are a variety of models at the moment in development such as the long range version of the TRIGAT and the incorporation of the MAVERIK with the AH-64 APACHE.

Although, not very widespread, gradually the need for a guarantee of self-protection for helicopters from attack by light air to air missiles is gaining ground. This being when they have the ability to destroy a large range of objectives. Among the

models in service we can find the French Matra ATAM MISTRAL, the United States FIM-92 STINGER and ADSM STINGER, the South African V3 KUKRI, the British STARTREAK, the Chinese QW-1 and the Russian SA-7 GRAIL, SA-14 GREMLIN, SA-16 GIMLET and SA-18 GROUSE. All of which are characterized by having a range of six kilometers, and include a light explosive head and infra-red unit to guide them up to the target, which could be a stationary helicopter or a transport plane in slow flight. The missile needs to be able to carry out quick maneuvres to reach the target within a reasonable time from being launched and to make impact.

Naval weapons

Submarines can be attacked when they are moving on the surface with machine guns, cannons and rockets although, usually they are submerged, for which special weapons are needed.

Four light torpedoes can be located in the side launchers of the various naval heli-

copter models, and launched in the area where the submarine has been detected. It then homes in on its target by various methods. The submarine can be destroyed either by a direct hit or by the torpedo exploding in close proximity. Among the diverse number of models in service, some which stand out are the United States Mk46 which in its 324 mm 5 NEAR-TIP model is widely used by Western countries; the advanced Mk50 employed by the United States Navy; the Swedish type 43 & 422, Italian A-244/S, capable of covering distances of 4 miles and, evolved from it, the A-290. The Russian RPK-8 ZAPAD and S-3V, the British STING RAY, the French MURENE.

Surface units can be attacked by a wide range of anti-ship missiles carried by helicopters, these being equipped with a guidance system which is directed from the aircraft or by a system relying on the missile's own warhead. In the latter case the missile is fitted with an independent guidance system which does not need any external assistance from the helicopter, instead guiding itself to the target. Among the first of these mentioned

ANTI-SHIP

With a range of some 20 kilometres the SEA SKUA missile is guided towards its target by using the radar signals sent and reflected back to the helicopter carrier, demonstrating its efficiency in the Falklands and Gulf conflicts.

(which have a range of less than 12 miles), there are particularly noteworthy systems such as the Aerospatiale AS15TT; the British SEA SKUA; the Norwegian PENGUIN, which is also used by the United States, and the Italian MARTE 2. Among second type (which have a range greater than 30 miles) some of the more outstanding ones are the AM.39 EXOCET, launched from the French SUPER FRELON; the British SEA EAGLE or the SEA KING, which is the version used by the Indian Navy.

MUNITIONS

From light 5.56x45mm shells up to 30mm, this range of munitions produced by the French company GIAT is ideal for use on the various helicopter mounts.